D1452832

Psychological Profiles of Conjoined Twins

PSYCHOLOGICAL PROFILES OF CONJOINED TWINS

HEREDITY, ENVIRONMENT, AND IDENTITY

J. David Smith

Foreword by Robert Bogdan

New York
Westport, Connecticut
London

Copyright Acknowledgments

The author and publisher are grateful to the following for allowing the use of excerpts from:

City bars wedding of Siamese twins. (1934, July 6). *The New York Times*, p. 19.

Rooth, J. (1911). The Brighton united twins. *The British Medical Journal*, 653-54. Reprinted with permission.

Every reasonable effort has been made to trace the owners of copyright materials in this book, but in some instances this has proven impossible. The publisher will be glad to receive information leading to more complete acknowledgments in subsequent printings of the book, and in the meantime extends its apologies for any omissions.

Library of Congress Cataloging-in-Publication Data

Smith, J. David, 1944-
    Psychological profiles of conjoined twins: heredity, environment, and identity
 / J. David Smith.
    p.   cm.
    Bibliography: p.
    Includes index.
    ISBN 0-275-92965-5 (alk. paper)
    1. Nature and nurture. 2. Siamese twins—Psychology. 3. Siamese
twins—Case studies.   I. Title.
BF346.S5S65   1988
155.2'34—dc19   88-1592

Library of Congress Catalog Card Number: 88-1592
ISBN: 0-275-92965-5

First published in 1988

Praeger Publishers, One Madison Avenue, New York, NY 10010
A division of Greenwood Press, Inc.

Printed in the United States of America

The paper used in this book complies with the
Permanent Paper Standard issued by the National
Information Standards Organization (Z39.48-1984).

10 9 8 7 6 5 4 3 2 1

To Walter H. Smith, Jr.,

my father

with thanks for helping me
to understand the importance
of thinking and acting
independently

We call contrary to nature what happens contrary to custom; nothing is anything but according to nature, whatever it may be. Let this universal and natural reason drive out of us the error and astonishment that novelty brings us.

—Montaigne

Contents

Foreword

This book returns us to an old tradition in the social sciences: using the unusual—the human anomaly—as a vehicle to learn about the ordinary. In the nineteenth century, Jean-Marc-Gaspard Itard spent five years of his life with Victor, the "Wild Boy of Aveyron," learning about the educability of intelligence. This strange child had been placed on public display after being captured by peasants in the woods in southern France. In the 1930s the sociologist Kingsley Davis reflected on the cases of two girls, Anna and Isabella, both of whom had been deprived of human contact during their early years, and illuminated how we are all profoundly social beings. More recently, Ashley Montagu pondered the question of the effect of ugliness on personality using the case of John Merrick, the Elephant Man, as data.

Biological variation and spontaneously occurring events help create unusual individuals whose differences highlight questions about the human condition that can't easily be seen or studied in typical folks. Some of these "human oddities" provide the equivalent of natural experiments—the "what if's" of human science. Those who pursue these natural experiments for the source of their data must have keen eyes. Strangely, although potential subjects may be strikingly different, they are not always easy to see. Of course I don't mean this literally; what I mean is that what can be learned from them is not always obvious. In addition, the pursuit of these subjects is often thwarted by research conventions that emphasize large sample size and quantitative methods. Keen eyes continue to be needed once a subject is found. The data is often thin, requiring extraordinary detective work to get to the bottom of things. There is then the question of what to make of it all—how to see through the details to the larger issues at stake. In *Psychological Profiles of Conjoined Twins,* David Smith has met the challenge of the tradition of studying the human oddity by creating a wonderfully readable book that makes a lasting contribution to the study of human behavior.

Siamese twins is the popular name given to people who are biologically joined. The condition is the result of the imperfect splitting of a fertilized egg that, if complete, would have resulted in identical twins. Thus, we have in these rare occurrences the intriguing combination of people with the same genetic configuration living in, as close as we could possibly imagine, the same environment. The partners in such configurations are often strikingly different. *Psychological Profiles of Conjoined Twins: Heredity, Environment, and Identity* vividly documents this obscure fact by exploring the lives of a number of pairs. David Smith mines this data, which includes anecdotal material as well as psychological tests, to contribute an exciting new voice in the long-standing debate between those who think that differences between human beings are most strongly determined by genetic factors and those who believe that the environment is the dominant force.

The theme of the book is straightforward. Human behavior is more complex than environmentalists, or geneticists, or even those who look for an interaction between nature and nurture suggest. Smith's concern is with freedom, with qualities that lie within the person but are not simply biological, that are fostered as well as constrained by one's surroundings, but are not determined by them. Individuals are something more than the products of nature and nurture. Smith calls this other factor *intentionality.*

Psychological Profiles of Conjoined Twins is both an essay on the human condition and an empirical study. Smith's brand of research is a combination of investigative reporting and critical reflection. His style and approach are innovative yet grounded in the best tradition of humanistic social science.

Robert Bogdan

Preface

The search for knowledge in the discipline of psychology has often taken the form of studying large samples of subjects. We have sought to understand human behavior by examining the usual, the typical behavior or traits of our subjects. Normative data thus comes to form the body of our understanding of the human condition. We rely on what we find to be true of large groups of people to guide our understanding, expectations, and predictions of individual characteristics.

In the study of child development, psychologists have collected data on the average age when various developmental milestones are usually achieved by large numbers of children. This data is then used as a standard by which the development of individual children may be compared. A problem or precariousness is then detected by reference to these established norms. Most parents have had the experience of having their child's growth and performance reported to them in terms of percentiles. When this occurs they are essentially being told how their child is doing relative to what is known of the typical child.

Abnormal psychology is the study of deviance from norms. The judgment that someone is pathologically depressed, or angry, or indulgent must be based on some conception of normality. Deviance implies a standard. The deviant is so judged according to our understanding of what most people do; by the ways that most people think, behave, or look. Without some concept of what is normal, abnormality would not be definable. Normality is the sum of our understanding of the usual, the typical, that which is true of most people.

The use of norms is reasonable and valuable. One of the foundations of medicine is the recognition of symptoms by the knowledge of health, by knowing the ways in which the body usually functions. Disturbed function can only be diagnosed by a comprehension of healthy body states. This knowledge comes from observations and recordings of the manner in which the various systems of the human body function in a normal state. Illness must be understood within the context of health. Defining health allows physicians to detect and treat illness.

There have been instances, however, when our understanding of the human condition has been advanced by studying exceptions to the norm. Sometimes we can achieve insights of substantial importance by notice of the unusual. Helen Keller taught us much about human potential. Work with Victor, the "Wild Boy of Aveyron," led to the development of important educational practices. The study of disease often contributes to our understanding of how to promote health. The study of psychopathology has resulted in most of our insights concerning the normal personality. This book attempts to better understand the lives of ordinary human beings by exploring the lives of some extraordinary human beings. Extraordinary in this context is meant to denote lives that are exceptional in the sense that certain physical, social, and psychological factors are radically different from those that are characteristic of most people. This book is about people who are referred to as conjoined or Siamese twins. The story of these people's lives is, I find, intrinsically interesting. More important, however, is the lesson that is embedded in their stories. I present here what I believe is an important metaphor; perhaps it is more than a metaphor. At times I am convinced that what I discuss here are data of the most compelling type. I will leave the judgment of metaphor or data to the reader. Before exploring the significant lesson I find in the lives of conjoined twins, however, I must briefly examine the scientific and philosophical context in which this study is grounded.

I became aware of the nature/nurture issue long before I was acquainted with the terms of the controversy. The concept that some human characteristics are inborn and others are learned probably comes early to most children. It may be that growing up in a southern state during the 1950s and 1960s made me particularly sensitive to the question of what people are born to be and what they become as the result of circumstance and opportunity. Whatever the influences of my own constitution, environment, and education, I know that the question of why people are different in their life conditions was one that was with me from childhood.

I was a psychology major in college. I remember being introduced academically to the environment/heredity question in my classes. Given my training and inclinations at that time, I was immediately drawn to the environmental camp. It seemed to me that the environmental position offered greater freedom in viewing the sources of human behavior. I remember the lively and good-natured debates I had with several of my professors during that period of my life. I must admit that I secretly prided myself on what seemed to me an ethically and philosophically superior stance. I was sure that people were primarily the product of their environments, not their heredity, and therefore, they were not the inevitable slaves of their genetic inheritance. If we would provide better environments for the nurturance of disadvantaged children we could overcome the inequities of the circumstances of birth. I was convinced that improvement of all sectors of humanity would result from the realization that "all men are created equal" and that only the different environments in which they exist make them unequal in skills, abilities, and characteristics.

It was years later that I recognized a basic flaw in my reasoning. I had been advocating the environmentalist position on the basis that it was the most sound argument for freedom in individual development. If environment was the critical factor, then people are born free regardless of race, class, or other family and cultural features. It was the environmental experience of the person that led to the particulars of that individual's attributes. People, from this perspective, are generally free of the dictates of genetics.

Through my role in teaching graduate and undergraduate courses to students preparing to become teachers and counselors, I finally came to a startling realization. I was teaching that people are the products of environment and heredity, with environment being the much more important factor. That was the total equation: heredity + environment = person. This, I realized, was my portrayal of the origins of all human actions and attributes. I believe this would be typical of the picture of human nature presented to most students in the behavioral/social sciences. The basic contradiction I discovered in my message to students was that I also taught that people are capable of change once they realize they are free human beings who can decide on the direction they wish their lives to take. The encouragement of self direction was (and is) fundamental to the theory of teaching and counseling that I deliver to my students. It became clear to me, however, that I was also teaching that people are passive products of factors beyond their control. I came to recognize that I was teaching my students to think of people as if they were determined yet to interact with them as if they were capable of exercising free will. I was shaken by this contradiction, this irony!

I came to face the reality that, although I obviously recognize the importance of heredity and environment in all aspects of human development and existence, I could not account for all that people become on the basis of those two factors alone. Although I had earlier cast my lot with the environmental camp because I believed it attributed greater freedom to the individual, I now understood that both genetic and environmental perspectives were essentially deterministic. Both views embody the concept of human existence that people are formed and controlled by forces not alterable by their own volition. I came to the realization that although hereditarianism and environmentalism are at opposite ends of a scientific spectrum, they share a common philosophical orientation in regard to human life. From either perspective, people are viewed as products. Both portray people as the products of impersonal forces and neither makes any allowance for self direction, decision making, or true intentions. Freedom, according to either point of view, is an illusion. What would appear to be decision making or self direction is merely the predictable manifestation of environmental or genetic programming.

The more I struggled with the intellectual conflict in which I found myself, the more I became convinced that intentionality—self direction—is as important as heredity and environment in determining the way we live our lives. Although severe genetic limitations and harsh environments may make it very difficult or practically impossible for individuals to exercise free will, it seemed to me that the potential for self direction, or choice, needed to be acknowledged as an equal factor in human development. Through my work with handicapped and socioeconomically disadvantaged people I had observed many instances of people transcending genetic limitations and environmental hardship. I was convinced that the capacity for freedom within the context of one's genetic makeup and environmental circumstances was real.

Still, I was not truly comfortable with my now more complex conception of the nature of human development and existence. It was more complicated yet, as I was attempting to convince myself, more comprehensive and correct. However, it was less supportable by the evidence of science I had been taught to value and respect. Particularly within the social sciences, I think, there is an almost defensive rejection of any ideas that cannot be tested and validated by what is acceptable as scientific methodology. Perhaps even more than in the "hard sciences" like physics and chemistry, there is a fear among social scientists of appearing to be "unscientific" in their work. Free will is difficult to define and measure scientifically. This is probably the reason that although I was giving much thought to this matter, I made very little mention of it in my lectures, and an occasional aside was the only reference I made to this matter with my students.

During a summer week of camping with my family I read *Celebrations of Life* by René Dubos. This passage from the book offered me both encouragement and discouragement concerning my questions about the role of will and choice in human life.

There does not seem to be any way to demonstrate scientifically that we are endowed with freedom. In fact, philosophical reasons make it likely that it is not possible for the human brain to achieve a complete understanding of its own working and that the existence of free will must therefore be accepted on faith, as an expression of the living experience. In any case, lack of scientific proof does not weigh much against the obvious manifestations of free will in human life and perhaps in other forms of life. As Samuel Johnson wrote two centuries ago, "All science is against freedom of the will; all common sense for it" (1981, p. 38).

During the summer of 1984 I participated in a course at Syracuse University taught by my friend and colleague, Bob Bogdan. Bogdan, a sociologist by training, has applied his talents to the study of attitudes toward and the treatment of disabled people. The course dealt with methods of qualitative research. In one lecture Bob explored the social phenomenon of "freaks." The theme of the lecture was that certain disabled people have been displayed for purposes more complex than the superficial reasons of amusement and curiosity of the crowds who have paid to see them. One of his points was that the exhibition of people as "freaks" serves to reassure the patrons of these shows of the distance between themselves and those people that they are viewing. As part of the lecture he showed slides and discussed in some detail the lives of certain famous "freaks." One of his examples was Chang and Eng, the original Siamese twins. I listened and watched with great interest. Their lives were fascinating. Of particular interest to me was the marked difference between Chang and Eng in personality and skills. They were born as identical twins and, attached at the chest, they spent every moment of their lives together. Yet they were very different. Several weeks later some questions crystallized for me. How could two people with identical genetic inheritance and as nearly identical environmental experiences as could be conceived be so different? By what mechanism were they different? The possibility of having discovered a focus for my musings on intentionality, on free will, on choice as a human capacity excited me!

I began to collect all the information I could find on the lives of Chang and Eng. Everything I found confirmed my initial impression of them. They were, indeed, very different individuals. In this process of information-gathering I came across references to other cases of conjoined twins. I started files on each of these cases and sought to learn all that I could about each of them. In every instance I found the same situation: Siamese twins were always very different in traits, temperament, and personality.

Chang and Eng were joined at the chest by a ligament-like appendage. It was about five inches in length, allowing them to walk side-by-side. They were discovered in what is now Thailand by an English merchant who brought them to the United States. They were exhibited extensively throughout North America. Eventually they were employed by P.T. Barnum who repeatedly toured them through the United States and Europe.

The twins eventually liberated themselves from their lives as exhibits and settled near Mount Airy, North Carolina. There they became successful farmers and were highly regarded members of their community. They married two of the daughters of a neighborhood family and both fathered large families.

Research on identical twins has often been used to bolster the argument that intelligence is determined primarily by heredity. The similarities in identical twins raised apart has been pointed to as evidence that the environment has little influence on the development of intellect. From a very different perspective, I think Chang and Eng are excellent subjects on which to base an examination of the role of intentionality as a mediating factor between heredity and environment. This book first focuses on and then flows from the story of their lives. What follows is a brief outline of what you are about to read. I hope that it will serve as a scaffold that will be helpful to you as you encounter the detailed descriptions and discussions that constitute this book.

Psychological Profiles of Conjoined Twins is introduced by a discussion of recent media reports of the births of conjoined twins. The contemporary view that twins born in this condition are severely handicapped and that only surgical separation can provide hope for normal existence is examined. Several examples of such accounts are presented and commented upon. Following these examples is a look at the carnival atmosphere that has long been associated with the occurrence of twins joined at birth.

The first three chapters of the book consist of a biographical study of the ''original'' Siamese twins, Chang and Eng. The opening chapter describes their lives from birth and childhood in Thailand to their fame as ''curiosities'' displayed by P.T. Barnum. The nature of their early lives is discussed in detail and the circumstances through which they became world famous as the ''remarkable Siamese boys'' is explained.

The twins eventually grew tired of being used as a display for the titillation of audiences and for the profit of their promoters. After breaking with Barnum, they toured independently for a period. Life for Chang and Eng transcended the sideshow, however, only after they settled in the foothills of the Blue Ridge Mountains. There, they became respected farmers and active participants in civic affairs.

Chang and Eng died in 1874. Eng awoke with apprehension in the middle of the night and found Chang dead. Within two hours Eng also died. Family, public, and scientific reaction to their death is an interesting story in itself. More fascinating and important in some respects, however, is the legacy of the descendants of the twins. A grandson of Eng, for example, became president of the Union Pacific Railroad. One of Chang's grandsons was an aide to Woodrow Wilson and later an Air Force general. The strength that Chang and Eng displayed in overcoming their own disabilities and in engendering strength in their families is exceptional.

Part Two expands the discussion of the life experiences of Chang and

Eng to other cases of conjoined birth. A number of instances of conjoined twins are discussed, some of which preceded Chang and Eng. Of
greatest interest, however, are those cases that followed Chang and Eng
but yet lived before surgical separation of Siamese twins became the
usual medical intervention. These cases yield the most complete
information on the lives of conjoined individuals. And, as indicated
earlier, they do prove to be individuals.

This section also contains a chapter on the history of literary interest
in Siamese twins. The discussion ranges from Mark Twain, who wrote
an essay on Chang and Eng and used accounts of their lives in a short
story, to contemporary writers such as John Barth. Particular emphasis
is placed on the interest that writers of fiction have consistently had
with reports of the individuality found within pairs of conjoined twins.
This recurring literary theme serves as an introduction to the third
chapter in this section, which is the keystone of the book. The striking
differences in personality, ability, and interests, which are characteristic of these twins, are discussed. These differences are documented by
historical accounts. More contemporary evidence is presented through
the results of psychological testing of conjoined twins.

Part Three is a discussion of the important philosophical and scientific questions that the lives of conjoined twins raise. The evidence concerning diversities in the lives of Siamese twins should cause us to re-
examine some of the prevailing assumptions in psychological research.
It should also provoke us to question the pervasive view that human
characteristics may be reduced to some simple ratio of heredity and environment. Research on identical twins has been used as one of the
strongest arguments for the hereditary nature of important human traits,
particularly intelligence. This section of the book includes an examination of the Cyril Burt affair in relation to research on twins and the
considerable influence that Burt's bogus research has had on social
science. The methodological weaknesses of other twin research are also
explored.

The final chapter of the book poses the idea that both hereditarian and
environmentalist views of the nature of human beings may be narrowly
reductionistic and overly simplistic. It is argued that another factor, intentionality, is critical in the course of human development. The active
participation of human beings in their lives influences the way in which
heredity and environment interact within an individual existence.

This, then, is the manner in which the message of the book is offered. I hope that this framework will prove to be helpful. I came upon the story of Chang and Eng, and subsequently the stories of other conjoined twins, as an unexpected source of important insights for me. I have been reminded that stereotypes so often blind us to the humanity of atypical people who are considered handicapped in some way. They also prevent us from learning about ourselves through them. I hope that I will prove to have been successful through this book in sharing the excitement and value of the insights that came to me in its preparation.

REFERENCE

Dubos, René. (1981). *Celebrations of life.* New York: McGraw-Hill.

Acknowledgments

The essential subject of this book is freedom. It is an examination of freedom as an integral element of the human constitution. It is appropriate then, at the beginning of this volume, that I should thank those who encouraged the freedom of thought and action that made it possible. This is no easy task and I only trust that while the frailty of my expression of gratitude will surely fall short of my true appreciation, my intentions will be understood by those people who have supported me as a friend and explorer in this endeavor.

My first expression of thanks is, as always, given to Joyce Smith. To her and to our children, Lincoln, Allison, and Sallie, I owe my greatest happiness in life. They have given me the inspiration and understanding which makes my work possible.

The course of the research for this book brought me into contact with several fine institutions. I was given very kind assistance by the staffs of the Southern Historical Collection in the University of North Carolina Library at Chapel Hill and at the Mount Airy Public Library. Bill McCarthy at Circus World Museum in Baraboo, Wisconsin, was particularly helpful in facilitating my work on conjoined twins.

My colleagues, Ed Polloway and Ken West, encouraged my work on this book when it was still in the thinking stage. They stimulated that thinking with both serious questions and with humor. Rosel Schewel and Pete Warren were also encouraging of my exploration of this topic from the beginning. Where some saw questions about the wisdom of pursuing an admittedly unusual subject, they saw potential value.

Thanks go to Carol Pollock of the Lynchburg College Library for her reference help with this book. She and the other members of the staff are an unfailing source of support and friendship. Lynchburg College also provided some financial assistance for my work on this project through the Committee on Faculty Research and Development. That award was received as both an expression of validation and a sign of confidence.

A special note of appreciation is due Bob Bogdan of Syracuse University. As I describe in the book, it was Bob who first inspired me to look more closely at the lives of Chang and Eng Bunker as expressions of freedom. Bob is a good friend and he has served as a valued teacher to me.

Several people I respect and trust read the manuscript of this book and offered criticism and observations which were of great help in preparing the final draft. Appreciation for their interest and efforts goes to Bob Lassiter, Tom Looney, and Tom Brickhouse.

Betty Shelton prepared the manuscript with exceptional skill and care. Her talent and dedication to quality in her work is remarkable. She has been a godsend to me in my writing.

Finally, I am grateful to be associated with senior editor George Zimmar at Praeger. His commitment to quality in this book has won my respect and gratitude.

Psychological Profiles of Conjoined Twins

Introduction

During the summer months of 1981 the *Washington Post* published a series of stories about the birth of a set of Siamese twins in Illinois. The first article reported that state officials were investigating the circumstances surrounding the birth of the twins. An allegation had been made that the parents had asked that the twins be denied food and water. The article also stated that charges of attempted murder were being considered against the parents and the medical personnel who carried out their request ("Charges Studied," 1981).

A second article gave greater detail. After the mother had been in labor for seven hours, two doctors were called in for the delivery. The birth of twins was expected. One of the physicians was the family doctor, the other an obstetrician. The delivery was difficult. A baby was born who appeared to be suffering from oxygen deprivation. The order was given to resuscitate the infant. But the obstetrician, noticing something that others in the delivery room had apparently not seen, immediately ordered that resuscitation be withheld and that the baby be covered. The father, also a doctor and in the delivery room, reportedly agreed with the obstetrician. The two of them knew what others in the delivery room had not yet realized, Siamese twins had just been delivered.

Later, according to a court report, the parents and the family doctor requested that the twin boys be given no food or water. This directive was apparently followed. At birth the Siamese twins had weighed nine pounds, twelve ounces. By the time that a complaint was registered with the Department of Children and Family Services and an investigation conducted, the children weighed only six pounds. The babies were removed from the hospital's intensive care nursery and placed in protective custody of the state (Wadler, 1981a).

In a subsequent custody hearing the presiding judge observed that there was no doubt in his mind that "all parties involved thought they were doing the right thing. . . . Anyone who has sat through this trial, unless they have a brick in place of a heart, must have compassion for all involved." He posed the question, however, of whether "our society [has] retrograded to the stage where we can say to a newborn abnormal child, 'You have no right to try to live with a little help from us' " (Wadler, 1981b, p. A13d).

The judge awarded custody of the twins to Family Services until another hearing could be held. He allowed the parents unlimited visitation rights. A grand jury continued investigations of criminal charges in the case (Wadler, 1981b).

A few days later the parents and their physician were indicted on charges of attempted murder and child neglect. The judge commented that, although the court does not make philosophical judgments, "the juvenile court must follow the Constitution of Illinois and the United States, each of which contains a Bill of Rights. These bills of rights give even to newborn Siamese twins with severe abnormalities the inalienable right to life" (Wadler, 1981c, p. A91).

A month later the criminal charges against the parents were dropped. The judge dismissed the case ruling that there was insufficient evidence against the parents and their physician (Wadler, 1981d, p. A12). Custody of the twins was subsequently returned to the parents. The state, however, supervised the children's care for a period of time.

In July 1981 the syndicated columnist William Raspberry commented on the case of the Illinois twins. His perspective is reflective of the contemporary opinion of many people that conjoined twins are essentially severely handicapped people.

> On the one hand, it is impossible for me to imagine other than a life of misery for the Illinois twins, inoperably joined. On the other hand, it occurs to me that the side-show freaks, once a standard attraction at carnivals, mostly didn't commit suicide, which

says that they must not have preferred death to even a grotesque life. On what ground would we make on their behalf a decision that they themselves refuse to make? (Raspberry, 1981, p. A19a).

A year later the twins were separated in a nine-hour operation at Children's Memorial Hospital in Chicago. They survived the surgery which only months before had been described as impossible in their case ("Siamese Twins," 1982).

In contrast to the account of the Illinois twins is the story of a mother who has struggled against her Siamese twin daughters being viewed as severely handicapped or as "freaks." In 1949 a set of twins joined at the head were born in Los Angeles. For almost two years they remained in a hospital where they were monitored and studied by physicians. Finally the doctor agreed that there was no way to separate the girls, Yvonne and Yvette. They had entirely separate brains but their circulatory systems were linked at their heads in a way that made surgery impossible.

The doctors advised the mother, Willa Jones, to give the girls up. They felt that Yvonne and Yvette should be institutionalized. They pointed out, for example, that a full-time nurse would be required to prevent muscle atrophy. It was predicted that the girls would never be capable of more than a rudimentary crawl. Certainly, they would never walk.

The most complete account of the lives of Yvonne and Yvette Jones is a profile written by Bella Strumbo. At the time that her article was published the twins were thirty-two years old. While researching the article, Strumbo found that the twins were almost unknown outside of the Los Angeles community where they lived most of their lives and in Augusta, Georgia, where they had lived for a few years and worked as gospel singers (Strumbo, 1981).

When Willa Jones went to the hospital to bring her two-year-old daughters home she was given not only a list of special equipment that her children would need but also a hospital bill for $14,000. She didn't have the money. The only advice given to Willa was that she might earn the money by exhibiting the girls in a sideshow. She refused this option initially but eventually found that this was the only way that she could pay the hospital bill and support her daughters. She signed a contract with the Clyde Beatty Circus. The contract stipulated that 30 percent of all earnings would be applied to the hospital bill. According to

Strumbo, the twins were a huge success with the circus. They were subsequently displayed in carnivals as well. Within two years Willa had paid her bill and she brought her daughters home (Strumbo, 1981).

As adults the twins told Strumbo that they are happy. They do not regard themselves as handicapped or deformed but merely different. They said that they do not feel self-conscious about their condition. Ms. Strumbo felt that they were telling the truth and that the twins were very well adjusted. In private they showed no signs of self-pity and in public they handled the curiosity, and occasional cruelties, with grace.

As children the twins did not attend school but received a basic education through volunteer tutors who came to their home a few hours each week. In 1967 they were awarded high school equivalency diplomas. "They did not attend public school, although they were both physically and mentally able, 'because nobody ever suggested it', said Yvonne. . . . They would still like to go to college someday, she added, turning suddenly shy. 'We'd probably do pretty good working with handicapped kids' '' (ibid., p. B3).

Willa Jones raised her daughters to think of themselves as individuals. They clearly regard themselves as two separate people. They emphasize their separateness in small but significant ways. Most notable to Bella Strumbo was their almost constant use of singular pronouns, even when speaking of something that applies to both of them. "I went to the movie last night" or "I was up early today" are the kind of statements most frequently heard from the twins. " 'I speak for myself, she speaks for herself,' Yvonne said firmly" (ibid., p. B3).

Willa Jones continues to worry about and struggle for her daughters. She believes that if they were given the chance they could be happier. "They have keen minds, and if they had educations they could work, be productive . . . there's nothing in their environment to stimulate their minds" (ibid., B7). Willa still receives occasional offers from people who are interested in exhibiting the twins. " 'My babies aren't freaks! Somebody from a state fair in Puerto Rico just offered to pay me $600 a week—if I'd let them show my girls in a tent! A tent!' She spits it out like a dirty word" (ibid.).

Conjoined twins are rare. Not as rare, however, as most people think. Informed estimates place the occurrence at somewhere between once in every 50,000 to 80,000 births. In the past, and this is true for the most part today, few conjoined children survived infancy. They have always been the subjects, partially because of their rarity, of great popular interest. The first autopsy performed in the New World was done on conjoined girls in Santo Domingo in 1533. It was conducted at the request of the priest who had christened the babies. He had remained uncertain from the time of their baptism until their deaths whether they were one or two souls. He hoped the autopsy would reveal the answer to his quandary. The autopsy showed that each child had a complete system of bodily organs. The priest apparently felt vindicated by this knowledge for having baptized the children as two individuals (Cassill, 1982).

Throughout history there has been much speculation on the cause of conjoined birth. Perhaps the earliest comprehensive exploration of this question was done by Ambroise Paré, the distinguished sixteenth-century surgeon. In his book, *Of Monsters and Prodigies,* Paré offered his ideas on the possible causes of the phenomenon. Among the explanations he offered:

- A demonstration by God of his power by sending things which are contrary to nature.

- A punishment by God for the wickedness of the mother or father.

- Coitus during a woman's menses.

- An overabundance of semen ejaculated during intercourse.

- Narrowness of the womb.

- Slothfulness on the part of the mother.

- Hereditary diseases or accidents (Guttmacher and Nichols, 1967).

By the middle of the last century physicians were speculating that conjoined twins were the products of a malfunction in the process that usually results in the birth of normal identical twins. It was assumed that twins that were developing from a single fertilized ovum first separated as individual embryos and then fused again to become conjoined twins. The essential idea was that twins of identical genetic makeup in the close proximity of the womb came to adhere to one another. In other words, the concept was that the twin embryos became "glued" to one another during gestation.

The current view is different. Most contemporary researchers think that conjoined birth is the result of incomplete separation of identical twins from the beginning of their development. Twins become united because in the process of the separation of embryonic cells a connection is maintained. Hence, some body parts remain connected and develop jointly up to the event of birth (Guttmacher and Nichols, 1967).

Conjoined twins may be attached to each other at any point on their bodies. The Illinois twins were joined at the lower trunk of their bodies. Yvonne and Yvette are fused at the head. Chang and Eng, the "original Siamese twins," were attached by a flexible ligament at their chests. Although the manner of connection may differ, the result is the same; two people are bound to each other. Over the centuries the bond between conjoined twins has been viewed as a curse, curiosity, or a handicap. Today we are most likely to see such individuals as handicapped, probably as severely handicapped. The perceived severity of this handicap leads to ethical questions such as the one discussed in relation to the Illinois twins. We are also still subject, however, to the perception of conjoined twins as freaks.

A few months after I started the research for this book a friend, knowing of my interest in Siamese twins, brought me an article. Mostly in jest he presented me with a copy of the *National Examiner.* While standing in the checkout line at a grocery he had noticed a headline about Siamese twins. The story was, in more ways than one, hard to believe.

As we have discussed, conjoined twins are identical twins. The article in the *Examiner,* however, described a bizarre incident involving a conjoined brother and sister, clearly not identical twins. The lead sentence of the article stated, "A pretty, dark-eyed, 14-year-old-girl has been made pregnant—and incredibly, the father of her unborn child is her Siamese twin brother" (Clifton, 1984, p. 27). In sensational language the article went on to explain how medical researchers from all over the world had become intrigued with the case. A Dr. Singh was quoted as giving background on the twins' lives. According to his account, the twins were born in 1970 to a woman who had been treated by a local doctor with herbs for infertility. "Consequently the poor woman ovulated in such great abundance that somehow two separate eggs fused. And it was those eggs that were fertilized and produced these unique male and female Siamese twins" (ibid.). The report became more bizarre as it went on. Dr. Singh was further quoted concerning the condition of the twins. He described the youngsters as "robust and healthy, although they were tragically joined at the abdomens. . . . Because of the position of their bodies it is quite difficult for them to walk, and consequently they are forced to spend much of their time reclining. . . . So perhaps this should not be viewed as all that surprising, considering the unique circumstances. . . . Unfortunately, the doctor added, the fact that they are connected belly-to-belly poses a particular predicament. As Indira grows great with child, will her swelling push her brother further away?'' (ibid.).

I have found nothing since the publication of the *Examiner* article concerning the case. Whether or not it was based on fact or some semblance of fact, however, is not really important to our present exploration. I cite the article because of where it appeared and the way in which it was written. I think it demonstrates that the public still has a sideshow curiosity about conjoined twins. Perhaps this is understandable. No, of course it is understandable. Conjoined twins are rarities that most people would naturally find either curious, or perturbing, or entertaining. My hope is that in this book we will find a quite different interest in Siamese twins. My goal is to present a story of the lives of conjoined individuals that will be instructive, a story that will demonstrate that there are lessons to be learned from their lives. Let us proceed by first looking at the life histories of Chang and Eng.

REFERENCES

Cassill, K. (1982). *Twins: Nature's amazing mystery.* New York: Atheneum.

Charges studied in twin starving case. (1981, May 20). *The Washington Post,* p. C5.

Clifton, L. (1984, December 25). Siamese twins make themselves pregnant. *The National Examiner,* p. 27.

Guttmacher, A., & Nichols, B. (1967). Teratology of conjoined twins. In D. Bergsma (Ed.), *Conjoined twins.* New York: The National Foundation—March of Dimes.

Raspberry, W. (1981, July 29). Life and death matters. *The Washington Post,* p. A19.

Siamese twins listed in good condition. (1982, July 24). *The Washington Post,* p. A2.

Strumbo, B. (1981, August 27). Sisters in a singular world. *The Washington Post,* pp. B1, B3, B6, B7.

Wadler, J. (1981a, June 5). Deformed Siamese twins: Should they live, who should decide? *The Washington Post,* p. A5.

_____. (1981b, June 6). After emotional hearing in court, parents lose custody of Siamese twins. *The Washington Post,* p. A13.

_____. (1981c, June 12). Siamese twins' parents charged. *The Washington Post,* p. A1.

_____. (1981d, July 18). Criminal counts dropped in Siamese twins case. *The Washington Post,* p. A12.

Part One

Chang and Eng

One

From Duck Eggs
to Barnum

Chang and Eng were born in Siam, which is now the nation of Thailand, in May 1811. The twins' mother's name was Nok; their father's name is not known. Their father was a native of China. Their mother was half Chinese (Graves, n.d.).

We can only imagine what the event of the birth of the twins was like for the parents and their neighboring villagers. Everything was normal about the newborn twins except one thing: the babies were not entirely separate. At the chest they were joined by a thick cord of flesh. Surely the village had never seen anything like this before. It must have been confusing, if not terrifying, for the parents and those close to them. Fear and superstition may very well have surrounded the experience of the birth. Somehow, however, the decision must have been made by the parents to spare the unusual infants from rejection, abandonment, or even destruction, and to accept them as their own and nurture them.

It has been suggested that the names given to the babies mean "left" and "right" in the Thai language. A more plausible interpretation is that Eng means "to tie strongly" and Chang means "pale." Perhaps these were descriptive names given as a portrait of the appearance of the children at birth, one brother tied by nature to a weaker sibling (Hunter, 1964).

Meklong, the village where the twins were born, was situated about sixty miles west of Bangkok on a river from which canals ranged through the town. The village consisted, for the most part, of primitive houseboats that lined the canals. The livelihood of many of the villagers was derived from fishing, raising ducks, and selling duck eggs. It was in one of the little floating houses of Meklong that Chang and Eng were born.

In their adult years, the twins had only vague recollections of their early years. They recalled almost nothing that occurred before the death of their father when they were eight years old. They did remember that people were always very curious about them, and that they attracted a great deal of attention wherever they went. After the death of their father and an epidemic of cholera, which killed not only people but ducks, Nok found it very difficult to support the twins and her other children. At first she attempted to make a living by selling oil that she extracted from coconuts. This was a very laborious task and her young children were not strong enough to be of much help to her. Next she tried bartering small household items in the marketplace. Apparently she was wise and skillful in her trading. She had soon saved enough to reestablish her family in the duck and egg business. In this venture Chang and Eng were most helpful. By the time they were fourteen they had been furnished with a small boat from which they peddled the ducks and their eggs. They were apparently shrewd young businessmen and bargained well on behalf of their mother. In addition, their constant navigation through the canals resulted in their becoming quite skilled as boatsmen and swimmers (Graves, n.d.).

In discussing the early life of the twins I have already made two references to a document by Graves and I have indicated that the date of the reference is unknown. Judge Jesse Franklin Graves (1829-1894) was a friend of Chang and Eng for many years. As a neighbor and confidant in their later lives, he recorded many of their recollections and accounts. His manuscript was found by a granddaughter of Chang among the personal papers of her mother, who was a daughter of Chang. These biographical notes were written after the death of Chang and Eng. They are a primary source of the twins' personal histories, as they were related to the judge through the twins' recollections and through other documented sources. The granddaughter of Chang gave the papers to the Surry County Historical Society in North Carolina, which has cared for the document since. It was with great excitement that I found a copy of these accounts in the public library in Mount Airy, North Carolina. There is no record of the exact dates when Judge

Graves wrote these accounts. From this point on in the book, when I refer to the Graves papers I will use only his name in the citation; please look to the reference page for the full credit, sans date, to the work of Judge Graves.

Chang and Eng learned a special method for preserving the duck eggs that they had been selling fresh. The method involved covering the eggs in salt, then in clay and ashes. This apparently rendered the eggs edible and savory for an extended period of time (Hunter, 1964). Their reputation as egg preservers, and (certainly of greater importance) as joined twins, brought them more and more into public notice in their native country. Eventually their fame reached the king of Siam and he summoned them to come before him in his palace in Bangkok. They appeared before the court of the king and were rewarded with presents from the throne. They also sold their acclaimed eggs in Bangkok at a price which allowed them to put their mother and siblings on a more secure financial footing once they returned home (Graves).

Chang and Eng were now known throughout Siam. The fact that they were to eventually become world famous was to result largely from a chance meeting with a Scottish merchant, Robert Hunter. He had established trade dealings with Siam and his company's ships regularly carried goods to and from Bangkok. He eventually made that city the center of his operations and came to regard it as his home. The story of his relationship with Chang and Eng has been told by one of Hunter's descendants in her interesting book, *Duet for a Lifetime.* Kay Hunter explains that the merchant first caught sight of the twins in 1824. He was crossing the river on his way home from work one evening when he thought he saw a strange animal swimming some distance away. It appeared to have eight appendages and two heads. The appendages moved in perfect coordination through the water. He followed the creature's movements until it came to a small boat and climbed over the side. Hunter then realized that what he had been looking at were two small, thin boys naked from the waist up. He was also amazed to realize that the boys were joined together at the chest. Hunter talked with and questioned the boys that evening.

A friendship developed between Hunter and the boys that was to last for years. He also took an interest in the rest of the family and often visited their floating home. The use of Chang and Eng for commercial purposes probably occurred to Hunter early in his relationship with them. What is known for certain is that within a year of discovering them he sought permission from the government of Siam to take the boys to England. His request was denied (Hunter, 1964).

Another opportunity for fulfilling his plans for the twins did not come to Hunter for several years. When it did come it was through his acquaintance with Abel Coffin, an American who was the captain of a trading vessel. Hunter discussed Chang and Eng and the matter of exhibiting them with Captain Coffin. After he had met the twins, Coffin apparently agreed with Hunter that such a venture might be very lucrative. Together they approached the mother of the twins with an offer to take the boys to America and England. They assured her that the twins would be well cared for and would be returned safely. A cash sum for their services was also tendered. The reluctant Nok finally agreed, seeing it as an opportunity for her sons to travel and learn of the world, and as a source of material security for her family. This time the government agreed to the request as well (Hunter, 1964).

Chang and Eng left Siam on April 1, 1829. They were seventeen years old. With Captain Coffin and Robert Hunter they sailed aboard the *Sachem*. Judge Graves offers an interesting account of the twins' recollections of their journey.

> They were leaving their home, their native land so dearly loved, the Temples of the "Golden Supreme" in which they had been taught to worship, their mother and all their kindred, to go upon an untried venture among strange people, wearing strange faces and speaking a strange language. To them all was strange indeed. . . . As soon as the novelty of their situation on board ship began to wear off and the tedium of the passage began to be a little felt, our youthful adventurers determined to undertake to acquire a knowledge of the English language. And with their accustomed promptness and resolution they made arrangements and immediately commenced the self imposed task. They pursued their studies with such intelligence and assiduity during the voyage that before it ended they had made very considerable progress in the acquisition of the language, being able by that time to read a little and to speak some few words but not enough to enable them to converse intelligently with strangers (p. 7).

On August 16, 1829, the twins arrived in Boston. Coffin and Hunter immediately began to make arrangements to exhibit Chang and Eng.

Illustration 1.1.　　A lithograph of Chang and Eng made during their first visit to the United States. From ''Account of the Siamese Twin Brothers,'' by J. C. Warren, 1829, *American Journal of Science, 17.*

They rented a large tent and launched a publicity campaign. They were advertised as the "Siamese Double Boys." People by the thousands came to see them, paying high prices by the standards of the time. Coffin and Hunter made huge profits from the exhibition. Chang and Eng received the share previously agreed upon and were apparently delighted with making money in quantities that they had never dreamed of before.

The twins were not only a success as an exhibit for the general public. They also aroused considerable excitement in the medical community. Physicians were quite interested in examining them, in offering their opinions of the condition of the twins and in suggesting what should be done concerning their condition. Chang and Eng were accustomed to this kind of professional attention and advice. In Siam doctors had proposed methods for separating them. These proposals had ranged from hanging them across a fine cord for an extended period of time (the cord would gradually work its way through their connecting band) to cutting the bond between them with a red-hot wire (Daniels, 1962).

John Collins Warren, distinguished professor of surgery at Harvard, examined the twins. His conclusion was that the connection between them was mostly cartilage with some blood vessels, lymph tissue, and nerves. He felt that surgical separation of the twins would be very hazardous and he advised against it. The closing words of his report included a poor prognosis for Chang and Eng, particularly since they had now been taken from their native land.

> The Siamese boys present, I believe, the most remarkable case of this "lusus naturae", which has yet been known taking into view the perfection and distinctness of their organization, and of the time they have lived. Their health is at present good; but it is probable that the change of their simple habits of living, for the luxuries they now obtain, together with the confinement their situation necessarily involves, will bring their lives to a close within a few years (Warren, 1829, p. 216).

After a few weeks of exhibition in the United States the twins sailed for England. They were received there with great interest and enthusiasm in October 1829. Once again crowds thronged to see them. Again also, physicians were anxious to study them. Their promoters were probably pleased to have doctors examine the boys since their reports inevitably lent credibility to the claims that they made about the unique and authentic connection between the twins. Physicians were often quoted in what appear to be promotional brochures. An example is a testimonial given by Joshua Brooks. I found the testimonial contained in the transcript of what was probably a promotional statement used at exhibitions of the twins.

Egyptian Hall, Piccadilly
November 24th, 1829

CHANG & ENG—Two youths born in the kingdom of Siam, whose bodies are, by wonderful caprice of nature, united together as one arrived in London on Thursday Nov. 19th, and on Tuesday the 24th professors of Surgery and Medicine in the Metropolis, as well as some other gentlemen of scientific and literary pursuits in order that through their reports (if favorable) the public may be assured that the projected exhibition of these remarkable and interesting youths is in no way deceptive; and further that there is nothing whatever offensive to the delicacy in the said exhibition.

These youths have passed their eighteenth year, are in possession of full health and extraordinary bodily strength; display all the faculties of the mind in their fullest extent; and seem in fact in every respect to enjoy a state of perfect happiness and contentment.

Having seen and examined the two Siamese youths, Chang and Eng, I have great pleasure in affirming they constitute a most extraordinary Lusus Nature, the first instance I have ever seen of a living double child; they being totally devoid of deception afford a very interesting spectacle, and they are highly deserving of public patronage.

(Signed) Joshua Brooks (Hale, 1830, p. i).

Chang and Eng were exhibited in London for several months and then in most of the major cities throughout Great Britain. This tour continued until the spring of 1831 and they did not arrive back in the United States until March of that year. They then embarked on a tour of larger American cities and towns that lasted through May 1832.

During this tour, life began to change for Chang and Eng. Captain
Coffin was now their sole agent. Robert Hunter had decided at the end
of their exhibitions in Britain to return to his business of trade between
England and Siam. As the twins grew in age, maturity, and sophistica-
tion, they became dissatisfied with the management and treatment that
Abel Coffin afforded them. They also expressed doubt about the
fairness of the financial share that they realized from their display.
They finally dissolved their business relationship with him. In a letter to
Hunter several years later they explained their action.

Augusta, Georgia
5th May

Robert Hunter, Esq.,
(Late from Siam)
28, Arundel Street,
London.

Dear Sir,

Your letter of the 19th November last, came to hand on
Thursday, having been forwarded from Boston by our friend
J. W. Hale.

We are very much obliged by the information which you
have communicated to us respecting our mother and also for
the kind expressions used by you concerning ourselves. From
the length of time which has elapsed since the date of your
letter we much fear that this will scarcely reach you in
time—but if it should, we are happy to be able to acquaint you
that we are in good health and good spirits and we are getting
along in the world pretty well.

Since June 1st, 1832, we have ceased to be under any arrangement with Captain Coffin—we had then attained the age
of 21 and considered we had fulfilled to the letter and spirit all
the engagements entered into between Captain C. and ourselves
at Siam. Although in Sept. 1832 when Captain C. followed us
to the western part of the state of New York he told us that the
arrangement with the Government was for seven years, and

that 2½ years was mentioned to our mother in order to quiet her fears and prevent any obstacle from being in the way of our leaving home with him. However, this kind of double dealing was but badly calculated to induce us to remain with him any longer.

We fear that the great rising of the waters in Siam were disastrous to you as well as to many others, but we hope to hear after sometime that you are doing well, and that you are "very rich" instead of being as you say you now are, "very poor", but we suppose you mean that you are "very poor" in comparison with what you once were. We are fully determined to go back to Siam but cannot at present fix any time.

We have enjoyed good health since we saw you and are now completely acclimatized to America. We have nearly completed the tour of the United States, being now in the 19th state of the 24 which compose the Union.

If you should be in England when this reaches London it would be very pleasant to us to hear from you again and you can address your letter to No. 13, Maiden Lane, New York.

We are anxious to dispatch this letter to you as quick as possible so shall not extend it. If you should return to Siam before you have an opportunity of hearing from us again, you will give our most affectionate love to our mother, brothers and sisters. We hope you will be able to see them.

If you should go to Scotland, give our very warmest remembrances to our friends of your acquaintance in that country. We feel truly grateful for your kindness in writing to us and beg to subscribe ourselves as most truly your grateful friends.

Chang Eng (Hunter, 1964, p. 65)

After their break with Captain Coffin, Chang and Eng went into business for themselves. With the money from a few exhibitions in New York they outfitted themselves for a traveling excursion of their own. With a buggy, baggage wagon, and three horses, they visited smaller towns where they had not appeared before. In 1835 they traveled to England and staged what were apparently very profitable exhibitions. While abroad they also toured France, Holland, and Belgium. In the spring of 1836 they returned to the United States where

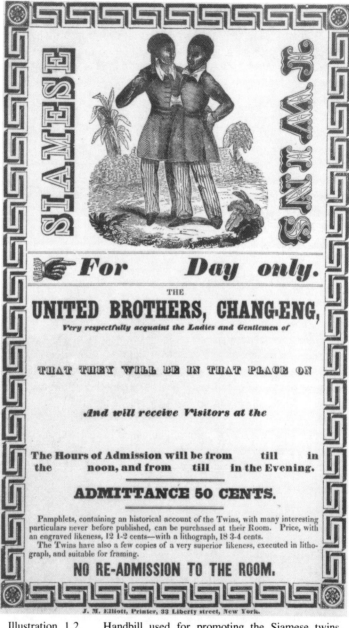

Illustration 1.2.   Handbill used for promoting the Siamese twins. Courtesy of the Southern Historical Collection, Library of the University of North Carolina at Chapel Hill.

they continued their tour of exhibitions, small towns in the summer, large towns in the winter, until 1840. It was also during this period of time that they contracted with P.T. Barnum.

Chang and Eng were already famous all over the world when they went to work for Barnum. Perhaps this is why he took little interest in them. Barnum apparently prided himself most on his "discoveries." The twins were not one of these. He was also irritated by their independence and shrewd business minds. It seems the dislike was mutual, for Chang and Eng avoided Barnum whenever possible. Nevertheless, the twins made a considerable amount of money while they worked with Barnum. The savings from this income would allow them to open a new and quite different chapter in their lives.

REFERENCES

Daniels, J. (1962). Never alone at last. *American Heritage, 17,* 28-31, 106-8.

Graves, J. F. (n.d.). *Life of Eng and Chang Bunker, the original Siamese twins.* Mount Airy, NC: Surry County Historical Society.

Hale, J. W. (1830). *An historical account of the Siamese twin brothers from actual observation.* New York: Elliott and Palmer.

Hunter, K. (1964). *Duet for a lifetime: The story of the original Siamese twins.* New York: Coward-McCann.

Warren, J. C. (1829). Account of the Siamese twin brothers. *American Journal of Science, 17,* 212-16.

Two

Exhibitions Now Farmers

After traveling almost constantly throughout the United States and Europe for more than a decade, Chang and Eng grew weary of that way of life. They were probably weary also of living life as exhibits. Surely they must have longed for greater privacy, greater normality in their daily lives, and acceptance as people rather than curiosities. They were to find these important elements for their lives in the foothills of the Blue Ridge Mountains.

The accounts of how they first arrived in Wilkes County, North Carolina, vary. One story says that they passed through the area on one of their tours and fell in love with the land and its people. Another account describes how Dr. James Calloway, a physician from the community, met the twins in New York while they were being exhibited by Barnum. He invited them for a visit and they were so impressed by what they saw that they decided that it was the place where they wanted to settle down. Regardless of the reason, by July 1839 they had established their home in this rural and isolated region. A letter to their old friend, Robert Hunter, reveals their circumstances and happiness in their new home.

                                        Near Trap Hill,
                                        Wilkes Co.
                                        N.C.
Robert Hunter, Esq.,   15th November, 1824
43, Corn Hill,
London.

Dear Sir,

   Your very kind and acceptable letter dated off St. Helena,
4th August last, was received by us yesterday, and we lose no
time in replying to it—thanking you very kindly for it. We
hope to hear that you have got safely to London and are much
gratified to have such a satisfactory account of our mother's
circumstances and health—but you forgot to mention anything
concerning our brothers. We hope you will write to us as soon
as you find leisure after the receipt of this. We have not
travelled any since the month of July, 1839, but we have
bought some land in this country, and raise our own corn and
hogs—we enjoy ourselves pretty well, but have not as yet got
married. But we are making love pretty fast, and if we get a
couple of nice wives we will be sure to let you know about it.
We weigh about 220 lbs. (together) and are pretty stout fellows
at that!!!! We congratulate you upon advancement in rank, and
hope you may continue prosperous. There have been dull times
in this country for two or three years past, but times are
improving now, altho very slowly. We live way off in the back
wood at the foot of the mountains called The Blue Ridge—in a
very healthy country within 25 miles of the State of Virginia
and fifty miles from the state of Tennessee.

   We have wood and water in great abundance and our neigh-
bours are all on an equality, and none are very rich—people
live comfortably, but each man tills his own soil.

   You will form a good idea of how much we are in the back
woods when we tell you that we are upwards of 300 miles
from the seaport town and 180 miles from any railroad. So we
are quite removed from the march of intellect.

   Give our best and kind remembrances to all our friends of
your acquaintance, in England and Scotland.

        Believe us to be
           Yours very truly and sincerely,
              Chang Eng (Hunter, 1964, pp. 80-81)

Using their savings from years of exhibitions, the twins ran a general store. They sold staple food goods and supplies. This business did not keep their interest for long. They soon decided to become farmers and came to be accepted and respected by their neighbors for their hard work and frugality. It was said of them that they could do the work of four. They used a special plow that was wide enough for the two of them to walk side-by-side as they worked in their fields. They devised a way for chopping wood that capitalized on their attached condition, each alternating with the other the chops of their axes. They were excellent fishermen and hunters, and were attributed the credit for killing a marauding wolf which had terrorized the area by carrying away farm animals (Daniels, 1962).

The twins attended church services so regularly that a custom seat was placed in the church for them. They enjoyed playing checkers and other games with their neighbors. They were very interested in local politics and participated regularly in the elections in their district. In short, they came to be valued citizens of Wilkes County, North Carolina. To the people there Chang and Eng were no longer freaks.

By the time that the twins settled in Wilkes County they had taken an American surname. They were Chang and Eng Bunker. There are several different stories of how they came to adopt that last name. One version has it that they were in line at the naturalization office before they realized that they would be required to give a surname before they could become citizens of the United States. Someone in the office named Bunker suggested that they use his name and they accepted. Another story is that Bunker comes close to the Siamese pronunciation of Bangkok, that they named themselves after the capital of their homeland. The best explanation, however, seems to be the one that Judge Graves offers.

> Probably in the year 1832 they formed the acquaintance of three gentlemen then living in the City of New York, Fred Bunker and William Bunker and Barthuel Bunker, residing at No. 41 Warren Street to whom they became very greatly attached and in whose families they spent some very happy times. So great was this friendship, especially on the part of Chang for Miss Catharine M. Bunker, his particular favorite in the family of his friends, that he at one time in his life duly made his will bequeathing all his estate to the object on which his affections reposed, and for

many years the testament was unrevoked—in truth it was never revoked until he loved again and not so much in vain. In honor of their friends Chang and Eng assumed the name of Bunker in 1840 (Graves, p. 10).

In their letter to Robert Hunter the twins alluded to romance and marriage. These matters must have been much on their minds. It surely was the one area of their lives that remained to be "normalized." There are several references in the accounts of their lives written by their contemporaries that suggest they had often been attracted to young women and that they made joking comments about being in each other's way when it came to romance. Eventually they found a means of getting out of each other's way, at least socially and psychologically, in their relationships with Sarah and Adelaide Yates.

David Yates was a neighbor of the twins. He was a farmer and part-time preacher. He and Mrs. Yates had a large family; Sarah and Adelaide were two of his many daughters. Mrs. Yates was an unusual woman. According to Judge Graves she was "about five feet seven inches in height and nearly nine feet in circumference. Her accurate weight was never ascertained for the reason that there were in that neighborhood no adequate means of weighing her. Several contrivances were resorted to ascertain her weight, but the nearest approach to success was by using two pairs of steel yards drawing together four hundred and fifty pounds which being firmly secured a sort of swinging platform was attached thereto. When this good woman stepped upon the platform both beams flew up; but the gentlemen engaged in the enterprise estimated that her weight could not have been less than five hundred pounds. She was unquestionably the largest woman in this state, perhaps in America" (Graves, p. 12). Kay Hunter relates the story that some years later Mrs. Yates preceded her husband in death. According to her story, upon death it was impossible to get her body through the doorway of the house until a part of the frame on each side of the door was cut away (Hunter, 1964, p. 82). Judge Graves suggests that Chang and Eng may have originally been interested and comfortable as frequent visitors to the Yates household because they shared with Mrs. Yates the understanding of an exceptional physical condition. "It was not so very strange then that Chang and Eng should visit one like themselves out of the ordinary course of nature" (Graves, p. 12).

In 1936 Sheppard Dugger wrote a booklet entitled *Romance of the*

Illustration 2.1.   Lithograph of Chang and Eng in 1839. Courtesy of the Southern Historical Collection, Library of the University of North Carolina at Chapel Hill.

Siamese Twins. In the preface to the booklet he claimed to have known the twins. He says that he was also assisted by their friends and relatives in reconstructing the story of the twins' lives. Even with his assurance that everything that he has written is accurate, it is difficult to view the following conversation as a literal record of an exchange between the twins and the Yates sisters. I do think that it is a good example of how the imagination was and is sparked by speculation concerning the relationship between the twins and Sarah and Adelaide. The conversation supposedly took place the first time Chang and Eng met the sisters. The setting is described as a tent where the twins were being exhibited.

Two young ladies, well dressed and attractive came in, walked up to them, and entered into a lively conversation in less time than it takes to tell it.

Eng said: "My brother wants to marry; and if any young lady here will have him, we will have a wedding today."

"It is he who wants to marry," said Chang, "and he is putting it off on me just to raise a conversation with you about love. He'd marry at the drop of a hat, and drop it himself, if he could get the ugliest girl in town to say yes."

"The reason I don't marry," said Eng, "is because I'm fast to him."

"The reason I don't marry," said Chang, "is because I'm fast to him. Isn't it a pity that neither of two brothers can marry, because he is fast to the other?"

"Indeed it is," said Sarah; "is there no chance for you to be separated?"

"The doctors say not," said Eng, "and each of us decided that we would rather look on pretty girls, with a lean and hungry lovelook, and continue to want a wife than to be in our graves."

"What a pity," said Adelaide, "that you who love ladies so dearly can't marry, and that two young ladies can't have such lovely husbands as you would have been."

"Good-bye," said the girls. "Good-bye," said Chang.

Eng said "Good-bye, my brother will be back to see you some day."

"If I come back," said Chang, "I will leave him behind, because he always monopolizes the conversation of the girl I love best."

Eng said: "To show that I want to be fair, I will let him take choice of you girls now, and if we get back, the other shall be no less a choice to me."

Chang chose Adelaide, and they parted joking as the young ladies left the tent.

When they went to their room that night, Chang said to Eng, "We will keep in touch with those girls, for they think more of us than we are thought of by all else in America."

"Maybe you are mistaken," said Eng. "It was only a show acquaintance, and they did not want to render things unpleasant by bluffing our familiarity."

"It was more than that," said Chang. "I felt the thrill of their sympathy deep down in my soul. Maybe they will marry us."

"Marrying with us is a forlorn hope," said Eng. "No modest girl is apt to marry, where the pleasures of her bridal bed would be exposed, as ours would have to be."

"Brother, you see it wrong," said Chang. "It is the refined (and those only) who can excuse whatever is necessary to become a mother. We are not responsible for our physical condition, and we should not have to die childless on that account. We will see again, the dear girls who talked so good to us today; and, through their love we may have children to carry our blood and image in the world, when we and their mothers have gone to the Glory Land."

"Brother," said Eng, "I never saw you so great a philosopher as you are now. Those girls inspired you, and when you go back to see them, don't fail to take me, and I will do my best in helping you win Adelaide, who sent that thrill to the bottom of your craw. I know you have sand enough in your gizzard to digest it" (Dugger, 1936, pp. 9-10).

The actual development of the relationship was probably far less fanciful than Dugger's account. Judge Graves says that the twins fell into the habit of stopping by the Yates home on their trips to and from the town of Wilkesboro. They enjoyed talking with Mr. and Mrs. Yates and their conversations often lasted late into the night. They were also frequent dinner guests. Eventually their attention turned to Sarah and Adelaide. According to Graves:

As their acquaintance became a little more familiar, they often devoted much of their time to the young ladies whom they entertained most agreeably with accounts of their adventures, and the amusing scenes they had witnessed—interspersed with very soft sweet music on their flutes—melody very greatly admired by the girls who had never heard such instruments before. Chang and Eng had known the young ladies nearly five years, and had become very much in love with them. They had not made any very marked demonstration and could not well form any opinion of the feelings of the young ladies for them. They finally determined to know the worst, and began to show such marked signs of interest as could not be misunderstood (Graves, p. 12).

Apparently these "signs of interest" were both understood and returned by the Yates sisters. The first public awareness of the relationships which had developed between them was when the twins were seen driving their buggy through town, Chang with his arm around Adelaide and Eng with his arm around Sarah. The news traveled rapidly and caused an uproar. Although the twins had come to be accepted in most ways in their community, the idea that they were involved with "normal girls" was unacceptable.

Objections were raised on the grounds that the relationships were improper at least, immoral at worst. Pressure was put on Mr. Yates to bring an end to the courtships. According to Kay Hunter some of Mr. Yates's neighbors became very aggressive in trying to persuade him to bring his daughters under control. Some of the windows of his farmhouse were broken and threats were made that his crops would be burned if Sarah and Adelaide continued to see the Bunker twins (Hunter, 1964, p. 83).

There is no indication that Mr. and Mrs. Yates ever approved of the romantic involvement of their daughters with Chang and Eng. Whatever their feelings might have been before the ire of their neighbors was made known, they did heed the threats and tried to persuade the young women to bring an end to their romances. They argued that any continuance of the courtship would bring disaster on everyone and that Sarah and Adelaide themselves would eventually be the greatest sufferers (Hunter, 1964).

All means of persuasion from the parents failed to change the daugh-

ters' minds and nothing that Sarah and Adelaide said could convince
their parents to give consent for them to marry the twins. Finally an
elopement was planned. Judge Graves describes the plan and the
marriage:

> Of course it was to have been kept profoundly secret. The plan
> agreed upon was this: For a time the matter was to be apparently
> dropped until the ensuing county court week when Esquire Yates
> who was one of the county Justices would go to Wilkesboro to
> assist in holding the court, then the parties at an appointed hour
> should meet at a ''Covenant Meeting House'' which stands on the
> hill near the South Fork of Roaring River, and there, their old
> friend Colby Sparks, the Baptist Pastor, was to be in waiting
> ready to perform the ceremony, easy to be done, before there
> could be any danger from pursuant. They understood pretty well
> there could then be no pursuit, for the irate father could not know
> of their flight in some time, and the mother who weighed five
> hundred pounds could not follow over such roads as lay between
> the Yates homestead and ''Covenant Meeting.'' The elopement
> was never consummated. The parents having ascertained that the
> daughters intended to marry, and that they would not be dis-
> suaded from their purpose, allowed them to be married at home
> on the 15th day of April 1843. The Rev. Colby Sparks performed
> the ceremony. The marriage was a private affair but the few
> friends who happened to be there had the good fortune to partake
> of a most elegant supper (Graves, p. 14).

There is no information available on which to base an understanding
of the conjugal arrangements made by the two couples. Obviously this
is a question which has excited much speculation over the years. All
reports, however, indicate that they were in fact two distinct couples,
with each pair of husbands and wives proving to be most devoted to
each other. Eventually, Chang and Adelaide had three sons and seven
daughters. Eng and Sarah were to have six boys and five girls. Their
reputations as good husbands and fathers grew as their families in-
creased in size. They continued to be respected as hardworking and
honest people. Perhaps it was this image of them which eventually
quelled the anger and resistance that some of their neighbors had
expressed concerning the propriety of their marriages.

As the families grew they found themselves more and more cramped in their Wilkes County home. Having heard of a farm for sale in adjoining Surry County, near the village of Mount Airy, Chang and Eng went to take a look. They liked the farm, bought it, and moved their families there. They soon built a second house on the property, about a mile from the original dwelling where they all lived at first. They then established a pattern to which they were to adhere for the rest of their lives. They spent three days at Chang's house with Adelaide and his children, and then three days at Eng's house with Sarah and his children. This schedule became an immutable rule in their lives. It was probably a means for each of them to exercise control, anticipate some certainty in their lives, and meet family responsibilities. From descriptions that are available it appears that each twin in rotation became passive when it was his brother's turn to be the active head of his household for three days. Judge Graves wrote that, "On Chang's days Eng surrendered up his will and allowed Chang to go and to do as he wished and on Eng's days Chang surrendered his will and allowed Eng to go and do as he wished. And from this rule and engagement from that time they were never known to depart up to the time of their death. No emergency in the families, no occasions, sickness, marriage or death could induce them to violate that compact" (Graves, pp. 18-19). I find it interesting that the twins devised this technique for insuring a form of alternating autonomy and that Judge Graves refers to the "surrendering of the will" that was necessary to allow it to function. This concept foretells of our discussion in a later chapter.

Although the twins had been retired from exhibiting themselves (or allowing themselves to be exhibited) for a number of years by the time they married the Yates sisters, they continued to be of interest to the public. Chang, Eng, and their families were living relatively quiet lives in rural North Carolina but newspapers and periodicals regularly ran stories on them. These stories were often sensationalized accounts of their lives. This was particularly the case in stories of their marriages to Sarah and Adelaide. The twins had sought an escape from exhibitionism when they established their new lives in the foothills of the Blue Ridge but this was never to be entirely possible for them.

Chang and Eng, however, soon found it was necessary again to not only abide the public curiosity which surrounded their lives but to participate in and profit from it. Perhaps because of the financial demands created by their growing families, they began to tour again as the

Illustration 2.2. Chang and Eng, their wives, and two of their children. Photograph courtesy of the Circus World Museum, Baraboo, Wisconsin.

"Siamese Twins." In 1848 J. N. Moreheid prepared a booklet entitled *Domestic Habits of the Siamese Twins*. In the introduction to his description of their lives Moreheid stated:

> The question is frequently asked, "What has become of the Siamese Twins?"
> It is with a view of answering this question satisfactorily that the present publication is made.
> The writer has been personally acquainted with them for several years, and has visited them frequently at their present residence in Surry County, North Carolina, on which occasions they furnished him with the greater part of the facts and incidents contained in the following pages.
> Theirs, it is supposed, is the first instance that any one has ever seen of a double living child; and it is improbable that such another will ever occur again.
> This pamphlet is respectfully dedicated to such persons as intend visiting the Twins, during the tour which they have in contemplation through the United States, and are anxious to obtain more information concerning them than it is possible to procure from a few minutes conversation in a crowded room (Moreheid, 1848, p. 5).

Included in the booklet are two drawings which are supposed to represent the residence of Chang and Eng when they lived in Wilkes County and the home they occupied in Surry County (See Illustrations 2.4 and 2.5). While these drawings depict very stately homes, the twins actually lived in much more modest abodes. Illustration 2.6 is a photograph of their homes in Surry County. The other house, according to all available sources was comparable. The drawings in the booklet were likely designed to add to the celebrity and intrigue of the twins.

In the Bunker papers, which are housed in the Southern Historical Collection at the University of North Carolina, is a memorandum of agreement, a contract, between Chang and Eng, and Edmund Doty. The agreement, made in 1849, stipulated that the twins along with Eng's daughter, Catherine, and Chang's daughter, Josephine, would be exhibited by Mr. Doty. Doty agreed to pay the twins at the rate of $8,000 per year for a period of at least eight months starting on April 25

Illustration 2.3.   Lithograph of Chang and Eng and scenes depicting their home lives in North Carolina. Courtesy of the Southern Historical Collection, Library of the University of North Carolina at Chapel Hill.

of that year. The contract assured the Bunkers of first-class accommodations and travel arrangements. They were also guaranteed that they would be exhibited for no more than six hours each day. They were also to be provided with a "proper servant" (Doty, 1849).

The practical reality of the twins' decision to return to exhibiting themselves is emphasized in Judge Graves's manuscript:

> Being exceedingly anxious to educate their children, especially their daughters, and finding that their income was likely not to prove sufficient for that purpose they began to think of exhibiting themselves again as a source of profit. It was disagreeable business to them. And their dislike of the business, their fear they might not make it successful and their reluctance to leave their families to which they were greatly attached had prevented them from travelling since their marriage. But now their very affection for their children impelled them to sacrifice their own feelings and to engage in anything not dishonorable, however unpleasant. Their old acquaintance Dr. Doty made them an offer for their services which they accepted. They soon after repared [sic] to New York under their engagement with him and were again put on exhibition after having been in retirement for twelve years. For some reason Doty was unsuccessful. They remained only six weeks and returned with Doty's note as the pay for their services. About one third of which they realized several years afterwards. On this occasion the two oldest daughters, sprightly little girls, accompanied their fathers (Graves, p. 18).

The unsuccessful result of this attempt did not deter Chang and Eng from trying again to provide for their families through exhibitions. Not long after their return home from New York they received another offer. For the next year they toured all over the United States and Canada. They took Catherine with them again but Chang took his oldest son Christopher. The proceeds from this tour provided them with sufficient funds for a while and they remained at home for the next three or four years (Graves).

The twins were to tour and exhibit themselves more and more in the future, however, even as they longed to be at home. A letter to Eng from his daughter, Catherine, is illustrative of the affection within the family, the families' yearnings to have them home and the concerns the twins had when they were away.

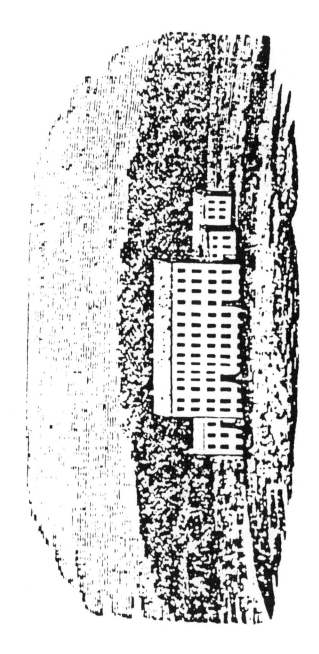

Illustration 2.4. From *Domestic Habits of the Siamese Twins*, by J. N. Moreheid, 1848, Raleigh, N.C.: E. E. Barclay. Original copy in the Circus World Museum, Baraboo, Wisconsin.

Residence of the Siamese Twins, Surry County, N.C.

THESE GENTLEMEN, AFTER TRAVELING EXTENSIVELY IN THIS AND OTHER COUNTRIES, FINALLY MARRIED AND LOCATED THEMSELVES ON A FARM IN SURRY COUNTY, NORTH CAROLINA, WHERE THEY AND THEIR WIVES ARE AT PRESENT RESIDING.

Illustration 2.5.   From *Domestic Habits of the Siamese Twins,* by J. N. Moreheid, 1848, Raleigh, N.C.: E. E. Barclay. Original copy in the Circus World Museum, Baraboo, Wisconsin.

Mount Airy
Sept. 15th, 1867

Dear Papa

We have just received your letter and the postage stamps, we are all very glad to hear from you. You said you was uneasy about home—there is no use for you to be so uneasy for Mama and myself will try and do the best we can, and I think the children will do the same. I wrote you about the 7th of Sept. I directed my letter to Nassua, N.H. Mont and Chris got home safe on Saturday about 10 o'clock. Mont says the tobacco is

Illustration 2.6. One of the twins' homes in Surry County. Penciled on the back of the photograph was this notation: "Where they lived and died—Eng Bunker and his Siamese twin built this home 100 years ago. The twins died in this house where Robert Bunker lives today." Photograph courtesy of the Southern Historical Collection, Library of the University of North Carolina at Chapel Hill.

very good, and they are doing very well with it. Chris has his barn up and is doing very well with it. Chris said he did not pay Mr. Palmer, but expected uncle to send him the money as he spoke of doing before he left home. Bud is nearly well of the Diptheria. Cleve Eller and Mr. Vanoy have been down to see us, they stayed one week with us. Cleve sends his best respects to Papa and uncle. We have very cloudy, and cool weather now. [At this point in the letter Catherine seems to speak to her father through her uncle. Perhaps knowing that they would always be reading letters together, she had become accustomed to speaking to both of them even though her letter was initially addressed to her father.] Tell Papa if he does not come home before the end of seven weeks that I do not think he will get many of the grapes to eat, but I am going to save him some anyhow. I can put up a big bottle full in liquor and sugar. I have already put up a jar of peaches in brandy and they are keeping nice. . . . Old Aunt Grace is here yet and does very well. Bobie is as well as ever and we are all about as usual. We hope this will find you all in good health, and don't be so uneasy about home, for nothing has happened since you left.

 Yours Truly

 C. M. Bunker (Bunker, 1867)

REFERENCES

Bunker, C. M. (1867). [Letter] Bunker papers (#3761). Chapel Hill, NC: Southern Historical Collection, University of North Carolina Library.

Daniels, J. (1962). Never alone at last. *American Heritage, 17,* 28-31, 106-8.

Doty, E. (1849). Memorandum of agreement. Bunker papers (#3761). Chapel Hill, NC: Southern Historical Collection, University of North Carolina Library.

Dugger, S. M. (1936). *Romance of the Siamese twins.* Burnsville, NC: Edwards Printing Company.

Graves, J. F. (n.d.). *Life of Eng and Chang Bunker, the original Siamese twins.* Mount Airy, NC: Surry County Historical Society.

Hunter, K. (1964). *Duet for a lifetime: The story of the original Siamese twins.* New York: Coward-McCann.

Moreheid, J. N. (1848). *Domestic habits of the Siamese twins.* Raleigh, NC: E. E. Barclay.

Three

The Legacy

The Civil War was a torturous ordeal for the United States in a myriad of ways. During 1861 to 1865, the years in which the actual fighting took place, the nation saw death and suffering among its people on a scale that had never before been imagined. The aftermath of the war was also devastating socially and economically to many people, black and white, northerners and southerners, the formerly rich and now poor, and the formerly poor and now destitute. The twins found that the Confederate currency they had saved was no longer negotiable. The market for the crops they raised was crippled. As difficult as it is to comprehend, knowing something of their backgrounds and sensitivities, they had also been the owners of a substantial number of slaves. Thus they lost what they had "invested" in human capital. Like many of their North Carolina neighbors, they found themselves in difficult times. Unlike their neighbors, however, they had a special option they could exercise in an attempt to overcome their new financial challenges. As undesirable as it must have been for the aging men, they turned once again to the business of displaying themselves as human curiosities.

Chang and Eng made several tours around the United States, each usually accompanied by one of his children. They invested the money they made during these tours well and were soon on a much more secure financial footing. During this period of time the twins also toured Europe in a series of successful exhibitions. It is their final visit to Europe, however, to which we will now turn our attention.

Chang and Eng left for Europe from New York aboard the steamer, *Allamanni,* on February 1, 1870. With them were Chang's twelve-year-old son, Albert and Eng's son, James, who was a little older than his cousin. They arrived in Europe on February 19. During the tour they visited Germany, Russia, Austria, Italy, Spain, and France. On July 30 they sailed to return home. On the seventh day of the voyage they were playing draughts with the president of Liberia, a Dr. Roberts, when Chang suffered a stroke. He was immediately paralyzed in his right side, leg, and arm. He showed no response to the medical attention given to him aboard the ship. When they reached New York the best treatment available was given him but he did not improve. When they arrived home Chang placed himself in the care of his friend and family physician, Dr. Joseph Hollinsworth. Dr. Hollinsworth was apparently no more successful than the other physicians had been in finding a treatment that could bring about any real recovery in Chang's health (Graves).

Judge Graves does not go into the details of the final days of Chang's illness and the final days of life for the twins. He does, however, provide a poignant profile of their courage in those last days.

During all of this time Eng was entirely unaffected, still retaining his usual health and his vivacity of spirits in a wonderful degree when his situation is considered. It was not expected that Chang would ever recover and Eng must have been under constant apprehension of his death at any time, and although the experiments which have been reported had never been made, yet they had been examined by the most skillful surgeons and physicians of the world whose opinions were almost unanimous that separation could not be made without fatal result and he must have known that the death of his brother would be the immediate signal for his own dissolution. . . . The earthly journeying of these wonderful men was now over and they had returned home to their friends to remain during the last days with those who loved and cared for them most until they should be summoned and that not unexpectedly to go upon "that journey from whose bourne no traveller returned" (Graves, p. 30).

The impression that one might have from Judge Graves's account is that the deaths of the twins followed fairly quickly after they returned home from Europe, and therefore not long after Chang's stroke. In fact

Illustration 3.1.   Chang and Eng in their later years. Photograph courtesy of the Circus World Museum, Baraboo, Wisconsin.

it was more than three years after the stroke that they died. It is staggering to think of the burden that Eng had to bear as he physically supported his disabled brother. With Chang paralyzed in both an arm and leg, it must have been quite taxing on Eng to compensate for his twin's impaired mobility. It must have also been a period of great psychological stress for both Chang and Eng. Chang was faced with the emotional consequences of a physical handicap. Eng must have been faced daily with the question of what would happen to him in the event of his brother's death.

At several times in their lives the twins had pursued the question of whether they could be separated and survive. During their final trip to Europe they had consulted with the most respected surgeons in several countries on this question. They found no surgeon who would give them any encouragement on the possibility of a successful separation. Part of their motivation for seeking a separation must have been their concern for the welfare of their families should both of them die.

In 1941 Arno Luckhardt, a physician, reprinted the autopsy report on the deaths of Chang and Eng which had originally been published in the *Philadelphia Medical Times* in 1874. That report provides many important insights concerning the circumstances concerning the death of the twins. The night before they died it was time for them to make their usual move from Chang's house to Eng's. They rode the distance between their homes in an open wagon. The weather was very severe. Chang had been suffering for several days with a cough and with pains in his chest. His wife felt that he should not expose himself to the weather but he and Eng insisted on abiding by their long-standing commitment to alternate homes every three days. The next morning Chang claimed that he felt better. That night, however, he experienced severe pains in his chest (Luckhardt, 1941).

The text of the autopsy report described in detail the events that followed:

> The twins slept in a room by themselves or with only a very young child present; and some time in the course of Friday night they got up and sat by the fire. As they were accustomed to do this frequently, nothing was thought of it by those of the family who saw them, even though they heard Eng saying he was sleepy and wanted to retire, and Chang insisting on remaining up, stating that his breathing was so bad that it would kill him to lie down. Finally, however, the couple went to bed again, and after an hour

or so the family heard someone call. No one went to the twins for some time, and, when they did go, Chang was dead, and Eng was awake. He told his wife that he was very "bad off" and could not live. He complained of agonizing pain and distress especially in his limbs. His surface was covered with a cold sweat. At his request his wife and children rubbed his legs and arms, and pulled and stretched them forcibly. This was steadily continued until he went into a stupor, which took place about an hour after the family were alarmed. The stupor continued up to death; according to the statements of the family, there were no convulsions.

Dr. Hollingsworth did not reach the house until after the death of both of the twins. He found the wives, and especially the children, averse to any postmortem being made, but, after much persuasion, obtained permission to put the bodies in a position to be preserved until he could obtain someone from Philadelphia to perform the autopsy. He placed the bodies, after they had been thoroughly cooled, in a coffin, which was put in a wooden box, which was, in its turn, enclosed in tin; the whole being buried in a dry cellar in such a way to be imbedded in charcoal (Luckhardt, 1941, pp. 117-18).

Considerable interest and controversy surrounded the deaths of the twins. Newspapers all over the world reported their demise. Their wives were, indeed, reluctant to allow an autopsy. Some press accounts claimed that this was because they wanted to sell the bodies of their husbands for profit. I have found nothing that would validate this accusation. In fact, the final conditions under which they allowed an autopsy to be performed specified limits to the procedure which would result in minimal disfigurement to their bodies and their safe return to Surry County for burial.

During the Thanksgiving holiday of 1984 I took my young son on a promised "adventure" to North Carolina. We rambled and stopped according to our impulses and fancies. As a secondary agenda, however, I had convinced him that a visit to Mount Airy was a good idea. In addition to his interest in seeing the "real" place where Andy Taylor and Opie used to live (Andy Griffith apparently created the name Mount Pilot, the town closest to Mayberry, by combining the names of Mount Airy and nearby Pilot Mountain), I had told him about Chang and Eng. He had come to call them the "special twins." It was with at least a little enthusiasm then, that he agreed to spend some of our time looking for the place where the twins were buried.

There is a worn historical marker at the side of the road in front of the old white frame Baptist church that Chang and Eng attended with their families. The graveyard where they are buried is behind the church. I had seen a photograph of the tombstone and I expected to spot it right away. I didn't. My six-year-old ran ahead of me toward the back of the small cemetery asking, "Where are the twins?" He found many stones with the name Bunker on them and at each one he asked if this one was "for" the twins. None of these were. It was obvious that these markers were "for" generations of descendants of Chang and Eng. After spending some time looking at these stones and searching for the one we had really come to see, my son was becoming bored and tired, and I was becoming discouraged. I could not imagine why we had not found what I knew was supposed to be there. As we left the graveyard, I turned to take one last look for the tombstone and there it was! It was at the entrance and we had passed it when we first entered. Even though I had seen the photograph, I suppose that I was expecting to see something more imposing. It is a large stone but apparently not large enough to fit the legend I was pursuing. As I thought about it later, I came to view our experience as reflecting the essence of the lives of the twins as I now interpret them. My son and I had passed by Chang and Eng without notice and had found their families. If they knew this I think they would accept it as a tribute. As I understand it now they lived much of their lives attempting to escape being legendary for their condition and striving to create a legacy of care for their families. Let us now explore that legacy.

Sarah and Adelaide Bunker had been married to Eng and Chang for more than three decades when the twins died. Sarah lived for eighteen years after Eng's death. Adelaide survived her husband by forty-three years. After the public interest in the death of the twins had faded, their widows lived quiet and private lives in their small North Carolina community. They were of interest now only to their families and neighbors. As remarkable as the twins were in their strength and ability to cope with their circumstance in life, these women must have been remarkable people as well. Their marriages were like none before or since. They somehow sculpted a normal and nurturing home life out of the unusual social, physical, and psychological conditions they faced. Sarah and Adelaide, along with Eng and Chang, raised large families of, what were by all accounts, healthy and happy children.

In their book, *The Two,* Irving and Amy Wallace traced the lives of the children of Chang and Eng. It is a fascinating account. Of Eng's eleven children, four died during his lifetime. Rosalyn died of an accident in infancy. Georgianna died of accidental causes at age two. Julia died of unknown causes at nineteen. Catherine, Eng's oldest child, died of tuberculosis when she was twenty-seven.

Eng's remaining seven children lived long lives. Stephen, a veteran of the Civil War, was left in charge of the farm upon his father's death. He died at age seventy-three, having produced with his wife, Susan, a son, Woo, who was retired as a night watchman in 1976 at the time the Wallaces did their research.

James and Patrick left Surry County after the Civil War and moved to Kansas. James became a farmer and lived into his eighties. Patrick married and had four children. Late in life he experienced difficulties and lived his final years in the county poor farm in Medicine Lodge, Kansas, where he died at age eighty-eight.

William made Mount Airy his home for his entire seventy-seven years. His granddaughter, Gladys, became a nurse and achieved the rank of lieutenant-colonel in the United States Army. She visited Thailand and was royally received because of her relationship to Chang and Eng.

Frederick moved to Missouri and, according to a descendant, was killed in a barroom fight in St. Louis. Rosella married a local man named Ashby. One of her sons rose to great prominence; more on him later. She died in 1941 at the age of eighty-two.

The youngest of Eng's children, Robert, married and had two children, Kate, who became a schoolteacher, and Robert, known as Little Bob. When Little Bob married and had twin boys, Robert asked him to name the boys Chang and Eng. Little Bob died in 1975, and one of the twins, the current Eng, inherited the family tobacco farm. His brother, the current Chang, is a career man in the U.S. Air Force (Wallace and Wallace, 1978).

Chang's oldest surviving child, Christopher, was almost twenty-nine when his father died. He had served in the Confederate Army and was captured and imprisoned in Ohio. Christopher married when he was thirty-seven. He and his wife, Mary Haynes, had one son, Christopher L. When Christopher L. grew up and married, the elder Christopher told his son that if he gave him a grandchild he would will him his 1,000 acre farm. If he did not have a grandchild before he died, he vowed that he would leave the property to the Baptist Children's Homes of North

Illustration 3.2. Robert Bunker, the youngest of Eng's children, who lived until 1951. The bed in the photograph is the one on which the twins died. Photograph courtesy of the Southern Historical Collection, Library of the University of North Carolina at Chapel Hill.

Carolina. Christopher Sr. died at age eighty-eight without his wished for grandchild. His estate went to the Baptist's Homes. A portion of it was used to build Bunker Cottage at the Kennedy Children's Home in Kinston, North Carolina.

Chang's oldest child, Josephine, died of an apparent heart attack when she was twenty-three. Nancy died at the age of twenty-six. Susan died in 1922 at the age of seventy-two. Victoria died in 1896 at the age of forty-four.

Chang's sixth child, Louise, was deaf. He made special provision for her in his will. Her husband, Zacharias Haynes, was also deaf. He taught at the North Carolina Institution for the Deaf and Dumb and Blind for thirty-two years. They had nine children; one became a state legislator, another a special education teacher, and a third, a bank executive. Louise died at the age of seventy-eight in 1934.

Chang's seventh child was Albert. He was attending Guilford College in North Carolina when his father died. He remained a bachelor until he was sixty-five, when he married a young woman who had been a music major at Meredith Baptist College for Women. He became the elderly father to the three daughters they produced. When he was eighty-five years old he drove one of his daughters to Duke University to enroll her personally. He died at the age of eighty-seven in 1944.

Jesse was born deaf like Louise. He studied at the Institution for the Deaf and Dumb and Blind in Raleigh. He later married, had children, and owned a farm. He was killed when he was struck by lightning at age forty-eight while working in his fields.

Chang's daughter, Margaret Elizabeth, was ten when her father died. She later married Caleb Haynes. They had eleven children, several of whom became very successful. One headed a textile company, another an underwear company, and a third became a major general in the Air Force. We will discuss his life more thoroughly. Margaret died in 1950 at the age of eighty-seven.

Chang's youngest daughter, Hattie, was five years old at his death. She lived until 1945. She was seventy-seven when she died (Wallace and Wallace, 1978).

George Franklin Ashby became the most acclaimed of Eng's grandchildren. Born on September 3, 1885, he was the son of Eng's daughter, Rosella. After attending high school in Mount Airy, he took a job with the Atlantic Coast Line Railroad in 1906 as a $60 a month clerk. In

1911 he went to work for the Oregon-Washington Railroad, a subsidiary of the Union Pacific.

From that time on he rose steadily in the Union Pacific organization. He left the railroad's operating department in 1933 to become assistant to the vice president. Four years later he was made assistant to the president and 1941 was elected vice president of the railroad.

After serving as executive vice president and member of the board for one year, George Ashby was elected president and director of the Union Pacific on February 1, 1946. Under his leadership the railroad flourished and received the E. H. Harriman Gold Medal for its safety record. Before he retired he was elected as a director of the Association of American Railroads. He died on May 16, 1950 ("George Ashby Dies," 1950).

Chang's most famous grandson was Caleb Haynes. He was born to Chang's daughter, Margaret, in Mount Airy on March 15, 1895. He attended Wake Forest University, where he earned a law degree in 1917. Later that same year he joined the army as a flight cadet. After training he was sent to France as a test pilot. During the Versailles Peace Conference he served as an aide to President Woodrow Wilson.

In 1942, the year he was promoted to brigadier general, he organized and commanded the Bomber Command of the China Air Task Force under General Claire Chennault. By 1943 he was the commanding general, First Bomber Command at Mitchell Field on Long Island. In 1949 he was assigned as deputy commander for services at the Military Transport Service. By this time he had been promoted to major general. During his career General Haynes received many decorations including the Distinguished Flying Cross and the Silver Star. He died on April 16, 1966 ("Caleb Haynes," 1966).

Popular interest in the lives of the twins and their descendants was somewhat renewed in 1952 when an article appeared in *Life* magazine. It was written by Archie Robertson who had decided to visit the home of the twins in an attempt to search for their descendants. Robertson described his trip:

Some weeks ago I drove down to the hilly country around Mt. Airy in North Carolina to talk to some of the descendants of those two men who were connected at the breastbone by a short, thick ribbon of flesh. I hoped to find some memories of the brothers as human beings, not as freaks on exhibition. I had been told that a set of twins had been born into the family, two normal boys named Chang and Eng for the original "United Siamese Brothers."

I found them working in a tobacco patch with their mother and father, the Bob Bunkers. The 11-year-old boys, greatgrandsons of Eng, stopped work, their faces touched with an Oriental-American blend of mischief. Their parents straightened up on their hoes.

"We're kind of busy gettin' these plants set today," said Bob, a round-faced, friendly man. "Maybe you could come around after supper. There's a old book the twins brought with 'em from over yonder."

That evening, in the living room of their four-room house covered with unpainted siding, I examined, but could not translate, the family treasure—a bundle of strips, with a beautifully written ancient script on them. There are only a few other surviving relics, such as a double-sized chair on which Chang-Eng used to sit before the fire, and a double-length gold watch chain which they used in common.

"I'd dearly love to know what's in that book," said Bob. He takes great pride in his forebearers and especially in the fact that their abilities were respected by the local people (Robertson, 1952, p. 70).

Robertson found and talked with several other of the Bunker descendants, including Woo and Christopher. His last encounter with members of the family seems, however, to have made the greatest impression on him.

Before I left I went to see Mrs. Katherine Marcellus Cross, a granddaughter of Eng, who lives with her husband in Eng's house. Mrs. Cross, a sparse, tall, friendly woman with spectacles, likes to talk about the twins.

"They used to say this here was the garden spot of creation," she said, repeating a phrase I had already heard several times. "Daddy used to say that he and the other children would look forward to the twins' coming home after a trip," she said. "Seems as if they were a little more generous with presents and pocket money than their wives" (ibid., pp. 81-82).

Illustration 3.3. Photograph with penciled inscription on back. "Woo, Doc Bunker, and Doc's sons." Photograph courtesy of the Southern Historical Collection, Library of the University of North Carolina at Chapel Hill.

Robertson goes on to explain that Mrs. Cross mentioned that her daughter was graduating from high school that night and invited him to come along. Dorothy Cross, the great-granddaughter of Eng, was not only graduating that night but was speaking to her class and their guests. Robertson said that Dorothy spoke with skill and polish but that his mind soon wandered.

> I thought of Chang and Eng, and the incredible adjustment they had made, first to each other, then to an alien civilization. . . . Chang-Eng were the only Siamese twins to marry and found considerable families. They wove themselves into the warp and woof of their adopted country and made a contribution which goes beyond the cold limits of . . . science into the warmer territory of human relations. They would never be forgotten. There would always be some who would think of them as more than freaks. They were very strong men to accomplish what they did. They were met at least halfway by the open-minded, unfrightened frontier people of North Carolina who accepted them.
>
> And one should not forget the role of the women; I thought as I drove home by the Baptist churchyard; the American wives who stuck to their strange bargains, and the Chinese peasant mother who long ago encouraged Chang-Eng to run, jump, laugh and play when they were tiny, before they knew they were any different from anybody else (Robertson, 1952, p. 82).

A more fitting conclusion to this chapter would be difficult to accomplish. Archie Robertson's words were touching when I first read them and they remain so. Still, I must share the content of a letter I received from a lifelong resident of Mount Airy who kindly responded to my inquiry concerning the twins and their descendants. This gracious lady asked that I not refer to her by name and I will certainly respect that request.

January 18, 1985

Dear Dr. Smith:

> In answer to your January 2 inquiry about the personalities of Eng and Chang Bunker I can only repeat the general impression I have from the traditions of the people of Surry. . . .
> I will say that Walter and Elizabeth Kempthorne, who re-

searched the twins for Wallace, came away greatly admiring them; and the descendants of Chang, who previously would not talk about their ancestry, came out quite openly for the Kempthornes which sort of surprised me.

Eng was the phlegmatic one and Chang, I would gather, was the more intelligent. Chang sent his children to college, both boys and girls, and they became more socially prominent—one was a long time resident of Mount Airy.

Chang's descendants, whom I knew better, were known for their wit. They became the prominent citizens. Descendants too, were known for their "Bunker temper." Whether this applied to Eng's descendants I do not know.

Eng's descendants became respected and prominent county farmers. As a whole they stuck to this.

A trait which one of Chang's descendants drew to my attention . . . was their talent for music which was passed on. All of the Mount Airy Bunker descendants were musical, and at least one of the Eng's is an accomplished classical pianist and a graduate of Duke. The Kempthornes agreed that the twins, even if they had not been conjoined, would have made their mark.

A county tradition is that Adelaide Yates, Chang's wife, fell in love with Chang, and had to persuade Sarah to marry Eng. It was the fact that both Yates sisters quarreled that helped lead to their building separate houses. Both families were distant to each other, and still are, I guess. . . .

Oh yes, going back to their talent for music, other than the Duke graduate I do not know very well the descendants of Eng, but Chang's descendants were very musical—two of his granddaughters sang well, another was an accomplished pianist and a teacher of public school music, one grandson plays in the Winston-Salem Symphony Orchestra.

All of the descendants are prominent and respected people.

Sincerely yours
(Personal correspondence, 1985)

Respected indeed. Every account I have found of the lives of the twins reflects the respect they earned during their lifetimes. That respect has been maintained through the lives of their families. As I have learned more about the twins, my initial fascination with them has become admiration.

REFERENCES

Caleb Haynes, 71, retired general. (1966, April 7). *The New York Times*, p. 36.

George Ashby dies; rail executive, 64. (1950, May 17). *The New York Times*, p. 29.

Graves, J. F. (n.d.). *Life of Eng and Chang Bunker, the original Siamese twins.* Mount Airy, NC: Surry County Historical Society.

Luckhardt, A. (1941). Report of the autopsy of the Siamese twins together with other interesting information covering their life. *Surgery, Gynecology and Obstetrics, 72,* 116-25.

Personal correspondence. (1985). Letter to author. Lynchburg College, Lynchburg, VA.

Robertson, A. (1952). Chang-Eng's American heritage. *Life,* August 11, 70-73, 77-82.

Wallace, I., & Wallace, A. (1978). *The two.* New York: Simon and Schuster.

Part Two

Curiosity, Fascination, and Inspiration

Four

Others

According to Frederick Drimmer, who wrote a fascinating book on "human oddities" entitled *Very Special People,* the Siamese are fond of saying that they have given the world three gifts: white elephants, Siamese cats, and Siamese twins (1973, p. 49). Because of their celebrity and, perhaps because of their relative longevity compared to other conjoined twins, the term which originated with Chang and Eng has come to be applied to instances of conjoined birth in general. Until recently the term implied cases of twins who were born joined in some fashion and who lived out their entire lives connected. Starting in the 1950s, however, the term became more of a diagnosis that indicated the need for surgical intervention. Today surgical separation of conjoined twins who survive birth is more the rule than the exception. Medical advances have enabled parents of these children to anticipate with optimism the possibility of longer and more normalized lives for their conjoined infants.

Prior to the development of safer and more effective techniques for separating Siamese twins, however, there were several cases of conjoined twins that were extensively documented. Like Chang and Eng, the people whose lives constitute these case histories offer us important insights. They also provide us with data on the patterns and themes which characterize the lives of people who lived in this condition. Furthermore, the nature of their lives challenges us to understand more of our own life experiences.

There are several accounts of conjoined twins which predate the life-times of Chang and Eng. One of the most famous cases is that of the Biddenden Maids. Mary and Eliza Chulkhurst were born in Kent, England, in 1100. According to some accounts they were joined at both the hips and the shoulders. They lived until 1134. When they died they bequeathed twenty acres of land that they owned to their church with the instruction that income from the property be used to provide bread and cheese "cakes" to the poor each Easter Sunday. According to George Gould and Walter Pyle, who wrote a study of medical anomalies shortly before the turn of the century, the cakes were still being distributed annually in the late 1800s. Each cake was pressed with an image of the Biddenden Maids which included their names, year of birth and age at death (1896, p. 175). Illustration 4.1 is a reproduction of a Biddenden Maids' cake.

Gould and Pyle expressed some skepticism concerning reports that Mary and Eliza were joined at both the shoulders and the hips. They cite several sources which indicate that it is likely that the twins were united at the hips but not at the shoulders. They feel that the women were independently formed above the waist with each having two arms. The impression that they were joined at the shoulder may have come from the habit of the women of walking with their arms around each other and subsequent artistic representations of them in that position. Illustration 4.1 may be viewed as an example of that kind of portrayal.

According to Gould and Pyle, when one of the Biddenden twins died it was proposed to the surviving sister that she be separated from her deceased sibling. She refused, saying, "As we came together, we will also go together" (Gould and Pyle, 1896, p. 174).

In 1701, conjoined sisters Helen and Judith were born in Szony, Hungary. Dubbed the Hungarian Sisters, they were exhibited in Germany, Italy, France, and Poland. At the age of nine they were placed in a convent where they lived until their deaths at age twenty-two.

During their exhibition tours the twins were examined by physicians and scientists. They were joined at the back in the lumbar region. Helen was described as the more active and intelligent of the two. Judith became hemiplegic at the age of six and after that became rather physically delicate and depressed. When Judith died of cerebral and

Illustration 4.1.   A Biddenden Maids' Cake, from *Anomalies and Curiosities of Medicine,* by G. Gould and W. Pyle, 1956, New York: Julian Press (original work published by W. B. Saunders in 1896). Reprinted by permission.

pulmonary problems, Helen sank into a state of collapse and died almost immediately after her sister (Gould and Pyle, 1896).

Although there are a few other cases of conjoined twins which preceded Chang and Eng, the information available on most of them is sparse. Of greater interest and value are the descriptions of Siamese twins who followed in life their namesakes. It is important that we discuss a number of these in some detail.

MILLIE AND CHRISTINE

Chang and Eng had already become legendary when Millie and Christine, the "Carolina Twins," were born. Black twins born into slavery on July 11, 1851, in Columbus County, North Carolina, the twins were first exhibited by their owner while they were still infants. The twins were more extensively connected than Chang and Eng. Rather than a ligament, they were joined from the lower ribs to the bottom of their trunks. Below the point of juncture they shared a common nervous system. Otherwise, however, they were complete and separate individuals (Drimmer, 1973; Sullivan, 1979).

While they were still infants their slaveowner sold them to Joseph P. Smith for thirty thousand dollars. Smith also bought the rest of their family thereby providing the girls with the continuing nurturance of their mother. He exhibited the twins throughout the Gulf States, advertising them as a "Double-Headed Girl" (Drimmer, 1973).

Smith hired a publicity agent to manage and promote the appearances of Millie and Christine. At the first opportunity the agent, according to the twins, "absolutely kidnapped us . . . stole us away from our mother, and bore us far away from friends, kindred, or anyone who had a right to feel an interest in us" (Sullivan, 1979, p. 48).

For the next two years of their lives, Millie and Christine were clandestinely transported and exhibited in state after state. They were eventually taken to England. There Joseph Smith, who had been searching for them since they were kidnapped, found them in the city of Birmingham. After a hotly contested court case (Smith claimed rightful ownership of the twins but England had not recognized slavery as a legal condition since 1833) he regained custody of the children on behalf of their mother. Before leaving England, Smith and the girls made a command appearance before Queen Victoria's Court (Sullivan, 1979).

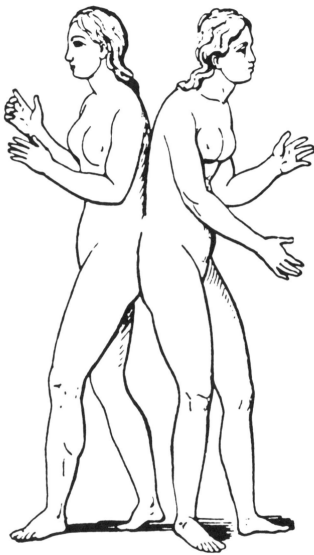

Illustration 4.2.   Reprint of the Hungarian Sisters, from *Anomalies and Curiosities of Medicine,* by G. Gould and W. Pyle, 1956, New York: Julian Press (original work published by W. B. Saunders in 1896). Reprinted by permission.

Illustration 4.3.   Millie and Christine. Photograph courtesy of the Circus World Museum, Baraboo, Wisconsin.

When they returned to the United States, Smith continued to exhibit the twins. Mrs. Smith (whom they came to call their "white ma") taught them to read and write, and to sing and dance. They became recognized as accomplished performers as well as "oddities." They had good voices and were sometimes billed as the "Two-Headed Nightingale" (Drimmer, 1973).

During the Civil War, Joseph Smith died. The aftermath of the war left Mrs. Smith in serious financial difficulty. Legally the girls had been emancipated and were free to leave. Apparently, however, they felt a loyalty to Mrs. Smith and stayed with her. They also returned with her to the exhibition circuit. Touring the circuit, they became very successful and earned as much as six hundred dollars a week. "We are interested pecuniarily in the 'show'," they said, "and are daily receiving and putting away our share of the proceeds" (Drimmer, 1973, p. 59).

In a 1969 interview, Mrs. T. Kenneth Cribb, the great-granddaughter of Joseph Smith, talked about her mother's memories of Millie and Christine: "They had independent minds, but they got along fine. One would carry on a conversation with one person and the other would be talking to someone else about something entirely different. But most of the time they acted like one person . . . " (Sullivan, 1979, p. 49).

Perhaps they did appear to others as one person in many respects. Even the billings, the "Two-Headed Nightingale" and the "Double-Headed Girl," detracted from the individuality that each of them possessed. But the ways that they found for existing with each other and as individual beings must have been complex and difficult to comprehend. The final words of tribute to them seem to me to be indicative of the complexity of their personal and coupled lives. After a long illness with tuberculosis, Millie died on October 9, 1912. Within seventeen hours Christine also passed away. They are buried in a churchyard in Columbus County, North Carolina, not far from where they were born and where they returned in retirement. Engraved on their tombstone are the words: "A soul with two thoughts. Two hearts that beat as one" (Drimmer, 1973, p. 61).

THE TOCCI TWINS

Although Millie and Christine were referred to as the "Two-Headed Nightingale," the closest approximation to a two-headed person in history were the Tocci brothers. Giovanni and Giacomo Tocci had two heads, two distinct sets of lungs, and each had a heart of his own. From the sixth rib down, however, they shared a single body. They had a single anus and penis, and only one pair of legs (Fiedler, 1978).

The Tocci twins were born in Turin, Italy, on July 4, 1875. They were only a month old when they were sent to the Royal Academy of Medicine in Turin to be studied. Soon they were placed on exhibition and created a sensation in both Europe and North America (Drimmer, 1973).

In 1891 the *Scientific American* published an article on the Tocci twins. It is an interesting account which includes a description of their differences:

> Their lives are distinct. They have regions of common sensibility, and of purely individual sensation. One often sleeps when the other wakes. There is no direct correspondence of their appetites. One may be hungry while the other is fast asleep.
>
> In their general appearance there is nothing repulsive. They have bright, intelligent faces, not of the peculiar cast common to cripples. They are educated and write their names as souvenirs for visitors.
>
> They are able to stand, but have not yet succeeded in walking, as each leg is governed by its own brain. The want of correspondence has proved fatal to any attempts in this direction. They can stand quietly, so that it is not only a question of strength. At their home they spend much time on the floor, using their inner arms for the most part, crawling and tumbling about and thus getting a certain amount of exercise. They can dress and undress themselves (p. 374).

The Tocci twins were sixteen when they toured the United States in 1891. They were promoted on that tour as the "Greatest Human Phenomenon Ever Seen Alive." It was reported that they earned a thousand dollars a week while exhibiting themselves on the American circuit. There are, of course, limits to the value that money can have to people who have been made into exhibits. According to Frederick Drimmer, the Tocci twins were interviewed during their visit to the United States by Allyn Hall, a longtime sideshow follower. They spoke to Hall candidly, explaining that their condition was a source of great unhappiness to them. They told him that they often felt discouraged and down-

Illustration 4.4.   The Tocci brothers. Photograph courtesy of the Circus World Museum, Baraboo, Wisconsin.

hearted. Hall described the boys as pathetic. After they returned to Italy from their American tour the twins refused to exhibit themselves again (Drimmer, 1973).

ROSA AND JOSEPHA BLAZEK

Rosa and Josepha Blazek were born in Skreychov, Bohemia, on January 20, 1878. They were normal and healthy except for being joined in the region of their buttocks. According to medical archival information, for the first month of their lives, their mother did not nurse them for she had been told by a midwife that they would not live. They must have been given other nourishment, however, for they survived and flourished. Later, on the advice of a physician, the mother did nurse the girls, weaning them when they were two years old (Perstein and LeCount, 1927).

The Blazek twins were displayed early in their childhoods, and were shown in sideshows and exhibitions for practically all of their lives. Josepha was quieter than Rosa. Rosa was, in fact, stronger and more aggressive in all of their activities. When the two walked, she was usually the leader. As with other conjoined twins we have discussed, one could sleep while the other was awake (Drimmer, 1973).

In their exhibitions the Blazek twins played violins and did Bohemian dances. Edward Malone, a follower of "freak" shows and collector of sideshow memorabilia has been quoted on the charm of the twins: "These two dames were like two Mae Wests, joined at the tail bone. . . . One would wiggle, while the other would waggle, and brother could they put on a great show" (Fiedler, 1978, p. 207). According to Signor Saltarino, a circus authority at the turn of the century, the Blazek twins had considered the possibility of marriage during the 1890s. He mused, perhaps somewhat sarcastically, on that possibility:

> We will not be able to blame the bridegroom . . . if he exhibits both of his wives for money. For he will have to provide double wardrobes; satisfy double appetites; fulfill double costly whims. . . . The future groom will have only one advantage over other men: he will have two wives—and only a single mother-in-law" (Drimmer, 1973, p. 83).

In 1910, however, the lives of Rosa and Josepha took a different turn. When they were thirty-two years old, Rosa gave birth to a child. The event, of course, attracted a great deal of public attention and generated a number of sensational stories. It was claimed that both sisters were nursing the child. It was said that the baby's father wanted to marry Rosa, but her parents would not consent. It was reported that a court refused to allow the marriage, ruling that the man would be marrying two women (Drimmer, 1973). A seemingly more reliable account of the birth, however, was published in *The British Medical Journal* that year. It provides a fascinating insight into this event in the lives of the Blazek twins.

> Last April, when old enough to know how to look after themselves, they made their appearance at the General Hospital, Prague. Rosa was troubled with an abdominal swelling. Then followed a delicate investigation of a type too familiar to all who understand female patients in trouble. When the possibility of pregnancy was suggested, both sisters gave "categorically negative replies." . . . Anyhow, Rosa must have been beloved, for before Professor Pitha could be summoned to the surgical clinic she was delivered on April 17th last of a fine boy. The mother and child are doing well, but sister Josepha, who was unavoidably present when Rosa was delivered, must be taken into account. Dr. Trunecek publishes a conjoint report of Rosa-Josepha, drawn up by Dr. Pitha when he examined the twins on April 29th, the twelfth day of the puerperium. He found that they were united posteriorly by the sacrum which was common to the pair, and by separate iliac bones. Accurate measurements of the pelvic inlet and outlet could not be taken; Rosa, the mother, clearly had a satisfactory pelvis, since it allowed of the birth of a well-developed male infant . . . milk was secreted by the breasts of both (p. 1313).

From 1910 to 1922 there was little recorded of the lives of the Blazek twins or of Rosa's son. In 1922, while on an exhibition tour of the United States, Rosa became ill with influenza. Three weeks later while she was recovering from this illness, Josepha had an attack of what was apparently appendicitis. Upon entering the hospital, Josepha was very ill but Rosa was feeling well. Josepha's condition grew worse. When it became evident that Josepha's illness was critical the question arose of separating the twins surgically for the possibility of saving Rosa's life. Before any action could be taken, however, Josepha died. Within twelve minutes Rosa was also dead (Perlstein and LeCount, 1927).

DAISY AND VIOLET HILTON

In 1911 a British physician reported on the birth two years earlier of a pair of conjoined twins who had come to be known as the Brighton twins. Excerpts from that report provide some basic information on two of the most interesting conjoined twins I have encountered, Daisy and Violet Hilton.

The case of the Brighton twins has excited a good deal of popular interest, and is, I think, of no less interest to the medical profession, as cases . . . who have survived more than a few weeks are extremely rare; as far as I can ascertain, in this country the case is unique.

The twins were born a few minutes before I arrived at the case, about 9 P.M., and the placenta had been expelled. The mother was a young primipara [first-time mother], aged 21, tall and well built. The labor, as described to me by the nurse, was almost uneventful; it lasted sixteen hours, and the pains were strong. . . .

The children, who are both girls, were well formed and of average size. I judged them to be fully 6 lb. each, and a few days later they weighed down the scales at 13 lb. The second child showed poor vitality from the first, and even now—two and a half years later—is neither mentally nor physically quite so vigorous as her sister. They were fed from the beginning on diluted cow's milk, as the mother declined to suckle them, and their feeding has not presented any difficulties. Their foster-mother, who took charge of them at birth, has only had to contend with aphthous stomatitis and a great deal of eczema intertrigo from the constant wetting and the extreme difficulty of keeping them both dry and clean. . . .

The union is fleshly and cartilaginous; it is very firm, and at birth allowed of little lateral movement; the children were almost back to back. . . . Now, at the age of 2½ years, there is much freer movement, and the children can turn sufficiently to fight or play with each other. . . .

At the present time the children . . . show no signs of being able to walk, or of any desire to attempt it. The utmost they can do is to stand propped up by a wooden framework which practically supports them. They are bright and intelligent, the elder one especially, and can talk as much as any child of their age. . . .

The question of the possibility of separation was raised at a meeting of the Sussex Medico-Chirurgical Society, and the unanimous opinion of all present was that it would be an unjustifiable operation, and would certainly result in the death of one child, and probably of both—an opinion with which, in view of our ignorance of the internal arrangements of the viscera and blood vessels of these children, I certainly agree (Rooth, 1911, pp. 653-54).

There are conflicting stories concerning the early lives of Violet and Daisy. According to Frederick Drimmer, the mother of the twins was an unmarried barmaid who sold the twins to Mrs. Mary Hilton when they were two weeks old. By age three they were traveling with Mrs. Hilton and her daughter, Edith, and performing in circuses, carnivals, fairs, and bars. The twins were taught to play musical instruments, to dance, and to perform acrobatic feats. When they were eight years old Mrs. Hilton brought them to the United States. Drimmer says that the girls were exploited by Mrs. Hilton and, after her death, by her daughter, Edith. Well into their adulthoods they were not paid by their ''guardians'' and severe restrictions were placed on their freedoms. Finally, in 1932, they spoke with a lawyer who became sympathetic to their plight. A trial resulted in a judgment forbidding further interference in their lives by Edith and her husband, and awarding them one hundred thousand dollars in damages (Drimmer, 1973, pp. 72-76).

Following the deaths of Violet and Daisy, however, an obituary in *The New York Times* did not make mention of these events in their lives. Instead it reported simply that:

They were born in England. Their mother died shortly after their birth, and their father was killed in World War I. At the age of 4, the twins were taken on a tour of Germany and the next year went

Illustration 4.5.   Violet and Daisy Hilton. Photograph courtesy of the Circus World Museum, Baraboo, Wisconsin.

to Australia, where they were exhibited in circuses and street carnivals for three years. They came to the United States in 1916 and about nine years later broke into "big-time" vaudeville ("Violet and Daisy Hilton," 1969, p. 47).

Whatever the facts of their early years may have been, they did eventually make it to the big-time. They were taught to dance the "black bottom" by Bob Hope and became friends with Harry Houdini. At the peak of their careers they earned $5,000 a week for performing. For a while they owned a hotel in Pittsburgh (Fiedler, 1979).

A series of newspaper articles during the heyday of their performing careers provide interesting glimpses of the lives of Daisy and Violet during those years. The first is a report of their involvement in a wedding.

Miss Mildred Elizabeth Wood, Daughter of Frank C. Wood of the State Normal School, will become the bride of Danny Van Allen Colbaugh, actor, Sunday night. Miss Wood will have as her maids of honor the widely known Siamese twins, Daisy and Violet Hilton.

The ceremony will be performed by Father James O'Neill in the Church of the Immaculate Conception.

For several years Miss Wood and fiance have been in the same stage show with the Siamese twins . . . ("Siamese Twins to Serve," 1934, p. 44).

Very shortly, however, news of the role of the twins in marriage plans was of a different sort. *The New York Times* reported that one of the twins had made application for a marriage license.

Miss Violet Hilton of the Hilton sisters, Siamese twins who do a dancing and saxophone act in vaudeville, failed to obtain a marriage license here and in Newark yesterday when she and her musical director, Maurice Lambert, applied for one.

Phillip A Hines, First Deputy City Clerk, was rather vague as to the reasons why he would not permit the marriage, but said he would leave himself open to criticism on moral grounds. He told Miss Hilton and Irving Levy, her lawyer, to take the matter up with the Corporation Counsel.

When the application was placed before Russell Tarbox, Assistant Corporation Counsel, he tried to dispose of it by writing across the top: "Application is denied on ground that bride is a Siamese twin," but Mr. Levy decided that was insufficient reason.

The case was then presented to William C. Charles, Acting Corporation Counsel. He merely approved the decision without saying why.

He did point out that the City Clerk was vested with discretionary powers in the granting of marriage licenses; may refuse them to ill, insane or other applicants, under the law, but admitted that there was nothing to prevent the marriage of a Siamese twin.

"But Mr. Levy says that he will take the case before the Supreme Court and seek a mandamus to compel the city clerk to issue the license," he was told.

"I think that if I had to oppose an application for a mandamus," Mr. Charles said, "I would raise the question of morality and decency."

The Hilton sisters left the Municipal Building after the license was refused and they and Violet's prospective husband journeyed to Newark to apply for a license there. City Clerk Harry Reichenstein turned them down.

"On what grounds?" demanded Violet's attorney.

"The same moral grounds as in New York," said Reichenstein.

Back at their home at 25 Central Park West the titian-haired sisters, who were born twenty-six years ago in Brighton, England voiced their indignation.

"If we don't get the mandamus here," said Violet, "we'll go to Elkton, Md. I know we can be married there." They cited cases of Siamese twins who had been married and raised large families ("City Bars Wedding," 1934, p. 19).

In the days following the denial of the license, newspapers reported on appeals to the decision. All of the appeals were unsuccessful. Violet and her fiancé were also unsuccessful in attempts to obtain a marriage license in several other states. Even Violet's confidence that she could be married in Elkton, Maryland, proved to be disappointing to her.

Attorney General Herbert R. O'Conor late today advised against issuance of a marriage license to Violet Hilton, right half of the famous Siamese twins, and Maurice Lambert after she had applied for a permit at Elkton, Maryland's "Gretna Green." He said it was "a matter of public policy." Applications for a marriage license have been denied the couple in New York, New Jersey and other places ("Bars License," 1935, p. 13).

Violet and her fiancé were eventually denied a marriage license in twenty-one states. Repeatedly the denials were based on the grounds that to allow the marriage would be a violation of moral standards. Perhaps the romance of Maurice Lambert and Violet died from frustration. They never married. A year later, however, Violet married James Walker Moore, a dancer. The ceremony was performed at the Texas Centennial Exposition (Drimmer, 1973).

A few years later Daisy married. *The New York Times* report gave details:

Daisy Hilton, 33, a Siamese twin, was married today to Harold Estep, 25, of Elmira, a master of ceremonies, whose stage name is Buddy Sawyer. City Judge Christy J. Buscaglia performed the ceremony in the office of the Chief Clerk of the City Court. Estep, his bride, and her sister, Mrs. James Walker Moore, who was married six years ago, are appearing in a show at a local night club ("Second Siamese Twin," 1941, p. 20).

The dateline for this news article indicates that the marriage actually took place in Buffalo. Perhaps officials in Buffalo were more open to the marriage of a conjoined twin than those in other localities had been or Violet's precedence had made the idea less unacceptable.

Although Violet and Daisy triumphed in being allowed to marry, neither of them found permanence or happiness in their marriages. Violet and her husband initially applied for an annulment after only a few months of marriage. A report from New Orleans described the request:

Harold J. Wining, New Orleans attorney, today filed a petition in Civil District Court asking annulment of the marriage of Violet

Hilton, one of the American Siamese twin sisters, and her dancer-husband, James Moore. Both Moore and Miss Hilton signed the petition. It asserted that the couple went through with a marriage ceremony as a "publicity stunt" in connection with Miss Hilton's appearance at the Texas Centennial and that they did not intend to enter "into a contract of marriage" ("Siamese Twin Asks," 1936, p. 16).

Ten days after his marriage to Daisy, Buddy Sawyer broke off his relationship with her permanently. "Daisy is a lovely girl," Sawyer said, "but I guess I just am not the type of fellow that should marry a Siamese twin. . . . As far as being a bridegroom under such conditions is concerned, I suppose I am what you might call a hermit" (Drimmer, 1973, p. 70).

The twins once explained how they managed their romantic involvements. Violet was quoted as saying that they learned "to get rid of each other. As Houdini taught us to do, we get rid of each other mentally. When Daisy had a date . . . I quit paying attention and did not know what was going on. Sometimes I read and sometimes I just took a nap. Even before that we had learned how not to know what the other was doing unless it was our business to know it" ("Violet and Daisy Hilton," 1969, p. 47).

Later in their lives fame and financial success escaped Violet and Daisy. For a while they operated a fruit stand in Florida. In 1960 they moved to Charlotte, North Carolina, where they found work in a supermarket at adjoining weighing counters. In 1969 they died of flu complications. The police found them lying on the floor of their home after they had not reported for work for several days. The minister of the Methodist church they attended in Charlotte said he knew of no survivors ("Violet and Daisy Hilton," 1969).

MARY AND MARGARET GIBB

Mary and Margaret Gibb lived as conjoined twins for fifty-four years. They came to prefer their condition over the alternative of separated lives. At a time when surgical separation was becoming a feasible intervention, they refused to discuss it. Even in the face of death they chose to stay connected.

Illustration 4.6.   Violet and Daisy Hilton. Photograph from ''Differences between Conjoined Twins,'' by H. H. Newman, 1931, *Journal of Heredity, 22*, p. 203. Reprinted with permission.

The Gibb twins were born in Holyoke, Massachusetts, on May 20, 1912. They were joined just above the buttocks. They had separate organs except for a shared rectum. Their circulatory systems were separate except for some minor arterial branches which connected.

While in their teens, Mary and Margaret appeared at Coney Island and performed in a vaudeville act which included playing the piano and dancing. For two years they appeared in Loew's theaters around the country. In 1930, they made a tour of Europe. From 1931 to 1941 they were with the Ringling Brothers and Cole Brothers circuses ("Gibb Sisters," 1967).

Several times while they were performing they made news by raising issues concerning whether they should be considered one person or two. The first incidence involved the question of payment for passage for their European tour. According to a newspaper report, the twins asked that they be allowed to travel on a single ticket with the White Star Line. They argued that they always traveled on a single ticket and had just arrived from Chicago by payment of a single railroad fare. Agents of the White Star Line responded that meals would be required for two persons and that two fares would be required ("Siamese Twins," 1930).

A second controversy involved the question of whether the Gibb twins should pay union dues as one or two performers. A United Press report indicated that they were considered as two.

> Siamese twins are two persons, not one, according to the advisory board of the A. F. of L.'s American Guild of Variety Artists. It decided that if Mary and Margaret Gibb, 27-year-old Holyoke Siamese twins, join the union each must pay a $10 initiation fee and $16 yearly dues.
>
> "Whereas the girls have two different names, they will have to join as two members," Thomas D. Senna Sr., New England representative of the union, stated.
>
> The sisters are now playing in Singer's Congress of Human Freaks at Boston Garden. The show manager, Herman Singer, had argued that since he paid the girls a single salary of $150 a week, they should be permitted to join the union as an individual.
>
> Whether the twins will join the union was not disclosed ("Siamese Twins are Two," 1939, p. 2).

I think that there is a strong probability that both of these controversies were generated by the Gibb sister's management for publicity purposes. There were stories during Chang and Eng's days of arguments over passage payments. The Hilton sisters were once involved in a dispute over union dues. These are the kinds of stories that the public has often found amusing and interesting concerning conjoined twins.

The physical health of the Gibb twins always differed. Their mother observed that from infancy there were noticeable differences in the girls in activity and vitality. At the age of thirty-four, Margaret had to have serious abdominal surgery which required she and Mary to be hospitalized for several weeks ("Surgery," 1946). Later Margaret developed kidney stones and had recurring kidney infections. Although both of them had problems with high blood pressure, Margaret's problem was more severe ("Siamese Twins," 1949, p. 9). Finally, in 1967, Margaret was found to have developed cancer. They dismissed completely the idea that they should consider surgical separation and the cancer rapidly spread to Mary. They died within two minutes of each other ("United unto Death," 1967, p. 50).

SIMPLICIO AND LUCIO GODINO

The Godino brothers were born in the Philippines on the island of Samar in 1908. They were also connected at the buttocks. By the time they were ten years old they had been brought to the United States for exhibition. While they were appearing at Coney Island, the Society for the Prevention of Cruelty to Children protested that they were without a proper guardian. Because of this protest, Louis Sullivan of the American Museum of Natural History had the opportunity to examine the twins. He was most interested in physical differences in the boys such as variances in height, head size, and fingerprint patterns. He found some differences and reported them in the *American Journal of Physical Anthropology*. He also included some general observations of the boys.

On the 31st of July, 1918, I had the opportunity of making a hasty and superficial examination of the so-called Samar Twins who until very recently have been exhibited at Coney Island. A satisfactory examination was made impossible by the fact that a legal controversy was in progress between the manager of the boys and

Illustration 4.7.   The Godino Twins. Photograph from ''The 'Samar' United Twins,'' by L. R. Sullivan, 1919, *American Journal of Physical Anthropology, 2,* p. 23.

the Brooklyn Society for the Prevention of Cruelty to Children. Mr. Arthur Towne, Superintendent of the Society, kindly gave me permission to make such observations as the twins would voluntarily submit to. . . .

The boys, Simplicio and Lucio Godino, are identical twins, in which the fission has been incomplete. The bodies are entirely distinct except for a juncture of the right buttock of one of the twins with left buttock of the other. . . .

Mentally the boys are normal in every respect. They are active and keen and show an intelligent interest in everything they see. They have evidently been well educated and have good command of the English language. Simplicio, the left twin, is right-handed and Lucio is left-handed (1919, p. 21).

As a result of the controversy about guardianship of the twins, they were adopted by the commissioner of the Philippines to the United States. Under his care, their education continued in both the United States and the Philippines. They were encouraged to develop their sports interests, despite their disability, and became very skilled in tennis, golf, and swimming (Drimmer, 1973).

When Lucio and Simplicio were twenty-one they again became the subjects of popular interest in the United States. News came from Manila of their weddings. They married sisters, Natividad and Victorina Matos. The Catholic ceremony was followed by a wedding festival at the home of their guardian, Tecodoro Yangco.

Their marriage had been opposed by a license clerk, who argued that the twins were one individual with a dual personality and that, therefore, the license would allow one person to have two wives. The Philippine Department of Justice, however, ordered that the license be granted ("Siamese Twins Married," 1929, p. 16).

The twins returned to the United States with their wives. The four of them went into vaudeville and became a headline act. Surely they must have been interested in generating interest in themselves and the following incident seems a likely publicity stunt. If it wasn't a stunt it must have been welcomed as a fortune of circumstance.

In 1929 this special report from Los Angeles was published in *The New York Times:*

Illustration 4.8.   Lucio and Simplicio with their wives. Photograph from "Differences between Conjoined Twins," by H. H. Newman, 1931, *Journal of Heredity, 22*, p. 201.

Because Judge William M. Northrup couldn't find anything in the law that permitted him to make the innocent half of a Siamese-twin combination suffer with the guilty half, the judge dismissed charges against Lucio Godino.

Lucio was arrested at a downtown intersection for making a left turn and other traffic violations. The astonished cops took him to jail in spite of the protests of Simplicio Godino, his Siamese-twin brother.

In the court the innocent twin told Judge Northrup that he wasn't guilty and didn't think he should be jailed or fined for what his brother did. The judge agreed (''Judge Releases Siamese Twin,'' p. 19).

Within a few years the trials of the twins became much more serious. In 1936 Lucio developed pneumonia. By the time that he and Simplicio were admitted to a hospital in New York his condition was considered critical. Simplicio showed no signs of the illness. At first Lucio seemed to improve with treatment. Within two weeks, however, he died. Forty-five minutes after his death surgeons performed an emergency opera-tion to separate Simplicio from his dead brother (''Siamese Twin Dies,'' 1936, p. 3).

For a few days Simplicio seemed to be responding well to the surgery. Daily accounts emphasized that his vital signs were all good and im-proving. During the surgery it was discovered that the only organ con-tained in the connection between the twins was a portion of Simplicio's large intestine; it was not attached to Lucio's body and was simply put in place in Simplicio's abdomen. Simplicio also seemed to be in a positive mental state.

> Considering his mental fortitude and his unimpaired health—the surgeons pronounced him physically stronger of the twins—no difficulty was foreseen yesterday in readjusting Simplicio to his new existence as a man who no longer has to walk backward when his brother walks forward, and who comes in adult life into first possession of his own initiative, instead of acting always under divided command (''Severed Twin,'' 1936, p. 8).

A few days later Simplicio died. His initially strong response to the separation weakened. He became unable to take nourishment and required transfusions. A spinal tap revealed that he had meningitis. He was soon overcome by the inflammation. The success of the first modern attempt to separate adult conjoined twins was brief ("Siamese Twin Dies After Severance," 1936, p. 28).

REFERENCES

Bars license to Siamese twin. (1935, January 26). *The New York Times*, p. 13.

City bars wedding of Siamese twin. (1934, July 6). *The New York Times*, p. 19.

Drimmer, F. (1973). *Very special people.* New York: Amjon.

Fiedler, L. (1978). *Freaks: Myths and images of the secret self.* New York: Simon and Schuster.

Gibb sisters dead; Siamese twins, 54. (1967, January 9). *The New York Times*, p. 39.

Gould, G., & Pyle, W. (1956). *Anomalies and curiosities of medicine.* New York: Julian Press. (Original work published by W. B. Saunders in 1896.)

Judge releases Siamese twin to avoid jailing his brother. (1929, October 12). *The New York Times*, p. 19.

Perlstein, M., & LeCount, E. (1927). The history and necropsy report of the Bohemian twins, Rosa-Josepha Blazek. *Archives of Pathology and Laboratory Medicine, 3,* 171-92.

Rooth, J. (1911). The Brighton united twins. *The British Medical Journal,* 653-54.

Second Siamese twin is wed. (1941, September 18). *The New York Times*, p. 20.

Severed twin lives but in odd world. (1936, November 26). *The New York Times*, p. 29.

Siamese twin asks annulment. (1936, September 10). *The New York Times*, p. 16.

Siamese twin dies after severance. (1936, December 6). *The New York Times*, p. 28.

Siamese twin dies but the other lives. (1936, November 25). *The New York Times*, p. 3.

Siamese twins. (1949, February 13). *The New York Times*, p. 9.

Siamese twins are two, union rules in dues test. (1939, November 19). *The New York Times*, p. 2.

Siamese twins have to book two passages on liner. (1930, March 7). *The New York Times*, p. 25.

Siamese twins married. (1929, July 14). *The New York Times*, p. 16.

Siamese twins to serve at bridal of stage pair. (1934, June 8). *The New York Times*, p. 44.

Sullivan, C. (1979). A strange kind of bondage. *American History Illustrated, 14,* 48-49.

Sullivan, L. (1919). The "Samar" united twins. *American Journal of Physical Anthropology, 2,* 21-24.

Surgery on Siamese twin. (1946, December 21). *The New York Times,* p. 21.

The accouchement of Rosa the Pygopaga. (1910). *The British Medical Journal,* May 28, 1313-14.

The Tocci twins. (1891). *Scientific American,* December 12, 374.

United unto death. (1967). *Time,* January 20, p. 50.

Violet and Daisy Hilton, Siamese twins dead. (1969, January 6). *The New York Times,* p. 47.

Five

The Twins in Literature

This chapter will serve as a transition from a general account of the lives of conjoined twins to a focus on the dissimilarities between people who are so connected in both heredity and environment. The themes that have been developed in literature about conjoined twins reflect some of the most basic questions and fascinations which I encountered as I began to study these special people. In both humor and tragedy Siamese twins have been used as vehicles through which to explore some of the most fundamental questions of human existence. Let us begin with humor. Mark Twain was fascinated with the lives of Chang and Eng. His satire on their lives is important enough to be included here in complete form.

> I do not wish to write of the personal habits of these strange creatures solely, but also of certain curious details of various kinds concerning them, which, belonging only to their private life, have never crept into print. Knowing the Twins, intimately, I feel qualified for the task I have taken upon myself.
>
> The Siamese Twins are naturally tender and affectionate in disposition, and have clung to each other with singular fidelity throughout a long and eventful life. Even as children they were inseparable companions; and it was noticed that they always seemed to prefer each other's society to that of any other persons.

They nearly always played together; and, so accustomed was their mother to this peculiarity, that whenever both of them chanced to be lost, she usually only hunted for one of them—satisfied that when she found that one, she would find his brother somewhere in the immediate neighborhood. And yet these creatures were ignorant and unlettered—barbarians themselves and the offspring of barbarians, who knew not the light of philosophy and science. What a withering rebuke is this to our boasted civilization, with its quarrellings, its wranglings and its separations of brothers!

As men, the Twins have not always lived in perfect accord; but, still, there has always been a bond between them which made them unwilling to go away from each other and dwell apart. They have even occupied the same house, as a general thing, and it is believed that they have never failed to even sleep together on any night since they were born. How surely do the habits of a lifetime become a second nature to us! The twins always go to bed at the same time; but Chang usually gets up about an hour before his brother. By an understanding between themselves, Chang does all the indoor work and Eng runs all the errands. This is because Eng likes to go out; Chang's habits are sedentary. However, Chang always goes along. Eng is a Baptist, but Chang is a Roman Catholic; still, to please his brother, Chang consented to be baptized at the same time that Eng was, on condition that it should not "count." During the war they were strong partisans, and both fought gallantly all through the great struggle—Eng on the Union side and Chang on the Confederate. They took each other prisoners at Seven Oaks, but the proofs of capture were so evenly balanced in favor of each that a general army court had to be assembled to determine which one was properly the captor and which the captive. The jury was unable to agree for a long time; but the vexed question was finally decided by agreeing to consider them both prisoners, and then exchanging them. At one time Chang was convicted of disobedience of orders, and sentenced to ten days in the guardhouse; but Eng, in spite of all arguments, felt obliged to share his imprisonment, notwithstanding he himself was entirely innocent; and so to save the blameless brother from suffering they had to discharge both from custody—the just reward of faithfulness.

Upon one occasion the brothers fell out about something, and Chang knocked Eng down, and then tripped and fell on him, where upon both clinched and began to beat and gouge each other without mercy. The bystanders interfered and tried to separate them, but they could not do it, and so allowed them to fight it out. In the end both were disabled, and were carried to the hospital on one and the same shutter.

Their ancient habit of going always together had its drawbacks when they reached man's estate and entered upon the luxury of courting. Both fell in love with the same girl. Each tried to steal clandestine interviews with her, but at the critical moment the other would always turn up. By-and-by Eng saw with distraction that Chang had won the girl's affections; and from that day forth he had to bear with the agony of being a witness to all their dainty billing and cooing. But with a magnanimity that did him infinite credit, he succumbed to his fate and gave countenance and encouragement to a state of things that bade fair to sunder his generous heart-strings. He sat from seven every evening until two in the morning listening to the fond foolishness of the two lovers, and to the concussion of hundreds of squandered kisses—for the privilege of sharing only one of which he would have given his right hand. But he sat patiently, and waited and gaped, and yawned, and stretched, and longed for two o'clock to come. And he took long walks with the lovers on moonlight evenings— sometimes traversing ten miles, not withstanding he was usually suffering from rheumatism. He is an inveterate smoker; but he could not smoke on these occasions, because the young lady was painfully sensitive to the smell of tobacco. Eng cordially wanted them married, and done with it; but although Chang often asked the momentous question, the young lady could not gather sufficient courage to answer it while Eng was by. However, on one occasion, after having walked some sixteen miles, and sat up till nearly daylight, Eng dropped asleep, from sheer exhaustion, and then the question was asked and answered. The lovers were married. All acquainted with the circumstances applauded the noble brother-in-law. His unwavering faithfulness was the theme of every tongue. He had stayed by them all through their long and arduous courtship; and when, at last, they were married, he lifted his hands above their heads, and said with impressive unction,

"Bless ye my children, I will never desert ye!" and he kept his word. Magnanimity like this is all too rare in this cold world.

By-and-by Eng fell in love with his sister-in-law's sister, and married her, and since that day they have all lived together, night and day, in an exceeding sociability which is touching and beautiful to behold, and is something to rebuke our civilization.

The sympathy existing between these two brothers is so close and so refined that the feelings, the impulses, the emotions of the one are instantly experienced by the other. When one is sick the other is sick; when one feels pain the other feels it; when one is angered the other's temper takes fire. We have already seen with what happy facility they both fell in love with the same girl. Now Chang is bitterly opposed to all forms of intemperance, on principle; but Eng is the reverse; for while these men's feelings and emotions are so closely wedded, their reasoning faculties are unfettered; their thoughts are free. Chang belongs to the Good Templars, and is a hard-working and enthusiastic supporter of all temperance reforms. But, to his bitter distress every now and then, Eng gets drunk, and, of course, that makes Chang, drunk too. This unfortunate thing has been a great sorrow to Chang, for it almost destroys his usefulness in his favorite field of effort. As sure as he is to head a great temperance procession, Eng ranges up alongside of him, prompt to the minute and drunk as a lord; but yet no more dismally and hopelessly drunk than his brother, who has not tasted a drop. And so the two begin to hoot and yell, and throw mud and bricks at the good Templars; and, of course, they break up the procession. It would be manifestly wrong to punish Chang for what Eng does, and therefore the Good Templars accept the untoward situation, and suffer in silence and sorrow. They have officially and deliberately examined into the matter, and find Chang blameless. They have taken the two brothers and filled Chang full of warm water and sugar and Eng full of whiskey, and in twenty-five minutes it was not possible to tell which was the drunkest. Both were as drunk as loons—and on hot whiskey punches, by the smell of their breath. Yet all the while Chang's moral principles were unsullied, his conscience clear; and so all just men confessed that he was not morally, but only physically drunk. By every right and by every moral evidence the man was strictly sober; and, therefore, it caused his friends all the more anguish to see him shake hands with the pump and try to wind his watch with his nightkey.

There is a moral in these solemn warnings—or, at least, a warning in the solemn morals; one or the other. No matter, it is somehow. Let us heed it; let us profit by it.

I could say more of an instructive nature about these interesting beings, but let what I have written suffice.

Having forgotten to mention it sooner in my narrative, I will remark in conclusion that the ages of the Siamese Twins are respectively 51 and 53 years (Twain, 1869, pp. 96-102).

I have found nothing which would indicate that Mark Twain actually knew Chang and Eng "intimately." I think it is clear that he based his fanciful, and very amusing, account of their lives on some of the information that had been published at that time concerning them. He took license with the facts in order to achieve his end purpose of the satire. He obviously created new characteristics for romance and marriage in the lives of the twins. There are other points at which he massaged the facts to fit the story he wanted to tell. Because it will be discussed later, one particular aspect of Twain's description of Chang and Eng deserves attention. His portrayal of the drinking habits of the twins is a reversal. Actually it was Chang, not Eng, who was a heavy drinker. Eng apparently abstained.

Twain retained an interest in Chang and Eng throughout his life. In 1889 he was persuaded on short notice to introduce James Whitcomb Riley, the poet, and Edgar Nye, the humorist, at a program of readings in Boston. Twain jokingly introduced them as "Mr. Eng Nye and Mr. Chang Riley."

I am very glad indeed to introduce these young people to you, and at the same time get acquainted with them myself. I have seen them more than once, for a moment, but have not had the privilege of knowing them personally as intimately as I wanted to. I saw them first, a great many years ago, when Mr. Barnum had them, and they were just fresh from Siam. The ligature was their best hold then, but literature became their best hold later, when one of them committed an indiscretion, and they had to cut the old bond to accommodate the sheriff.

In intellectual matters Mr. Eng Nye was always the dynamo, and Mr. Chang Riley was always the motor. Mr. Eng Nye had a stately intellect, but couldn't make it go, and at the same time Mr. Chang Riley hadn't but could. That is to say, that while Mr. Chang Riley couldn't think things himself, he had a marvelous natural grace in setting them down and weaving them together when his pal furnished the raw material.

So they worked together in that way. Thus, working together, they made a strong team; laboring together, they could do miracles; but break the circuit, and both were impotent at once. It has remained so to this day; they must travel together, conspire together, beguile together, hoe, and plant, and plough, and reap, and sell their public together, or there's no result (Fatout, 1976, pp. 238-39).

In 1906, to entertain his guests at a New Year's Eve dinner party, Mark Twain put on a performance with the assistance of a young man who, like himself, was dressed in white. The two of them had their arms around each other, and they were tied together by a pink sash to symbolize the connection between Chang and Eng.

We come from afar. We come from very far; very far indeed—as far as New Jersey. We are the Siamese twins, but we have been in this country long enough to know something of your customs, and we have learned as much of your language as it is written and spoken as—well—as the newspapers.

We are so much to each other, my brother and I, that what I eat nourishes him and what he drinks—ahem!—nourishes me. I often eat when I don't really want to because he is hungry, and, of course, I need hardly tell you that he often drinks when I am not thirsty.

I am sorry to say that he is a confirmed consumer of liquor— liquor, that awful, awful curse—while I, from principle, and also from the fact that I don't like the taste, never touch a drop.

It has often been a source of considerable annoyance to me, when going about the country lecturing on temperance, to find myself at the head of a procession of white-ribbon people so drunk I couldn't see. But I am thankful to say that my brother has reformed. [The Siamese brother surreptitiously takes a drink from a flask] He hasn't touched a drop in three years. [The twin takes another drink] He never will touch a drop. [Another drink]

Thank God for that. [Several drinks] And if, by exhibiting my brother to you, I can save any of you people here from the horrible curse of the demon rum, I shall be satisfied. [Twain hiccoughs] Zish is wonderful reform—[Another drink]

Wondr'l 'form we are 'gaged in. Glorious work—we doin' glorious work—glori-o-u-s work. Best work ever done, my brother and work of reform, reform work, glorious work. I don' feel jus' right (Fatout, 1976, pp. 541-42).

Although Twain was obviously fascinated with Chang and Eng, another pair of conjoined twins were to prove to be more influential on his work. Eventually this influence was evidenced in his story, *Those Extraordinary Twins.* The development of that story and of Twain's attempt to use conjoined twins as a focus for a major work is fascinating.

Pudd'nhead Wilson is a novel set in the Mississippi valley. Two baby boys are born in the same house, on the same day in Dawson's Landing, Missouri. One of these children is heir to the family fortune. The other is the son of one of the family's slaves, a beautiful woman named Roxana. The mother of the infant heir dies shortly after his birth and the care of both children becomes Roxana's responsibility.

Roxana is only one-sixteenth black but that one-sixteenth, as Twain points out, is enough to make her a slave. Her son is only one-thirty-second black and has blue eyes and a fair complexion. He can only be distinguished from the infant heir by his clothing, yet he is treated as property and it is made known to Roxana that her baby is subject to being sold. To save her son from slavery and separation she switches the infants. Nobody detects the switch.

The novel is a humorous and provocative tale of confused identity and of the arbitrary nature of the slave-master relationship. As the story develops, however, two characters enter who seem to be literally "out of place." Two identical twins, named Luigi and Angelo Capello, come to settle in Dawson's Landing. They are Italian aristocrats who are charming, educated, and talented. They are soon perceived as a threat to the male social hierarchy of the town. They become involved in a court trial, public disputes, and a duel. They eventually become the witnesses and suspects in a murder. Literary scholars have observed that the appearance of the twins in the novel is curious (Miller, 1983).

Twain wrote an appendix entitled "Those Extraordinary Twins" for *Pudd'nhead Wilson* which appears in several editions of the book. In it he explains that the novel was originally conceived as a farce based on the Tocci twins. He set out to write comic episodes grounded in the condition of Giovanni and Giacomo. Twain also explains that as he wrote the story the characters and plot got out of hand. The theme of senseless racial bigotry overcame the story of the conjoined twins (Twain, 1893).

In "Those Extraordinary Twins," Twain says that he had seen a picture of a "youthful Italian 'freak'—or 'freaks'—which was—or which were—on exhibition in our cities—a combination consisting of two heads and four arms joined to a single body and a single pair of legs . . . " (pp. 208-209). Robert Wiggins has argued convincingly that the picture that sparked Twain's interest was in the 1891 issue of *Scientific American* cited in the last chapter. Apparently he customarily had periodicals sent to him when he traveled abroad, and it was during one of his European tours that he learned of the Tocci twins (1951).

In 1895 a stage adaptation of *Pudd'nhead Wilson* by Frank Mayo opened in New York. After several performances, Mark Twain attended and spoke to the audience following the third act. His comments provide some insights concerning the place of the Tocci twins in the development of the novel.

> I am gratified to see that Mr. Mayo has been able to manage those difficult twins. I tried, but in my hands they failed. Year before last there was an Italian freak on exhibition in Philadelphia who was an exaggeration of the Siamese twins. This freak had one body, one pair of legs, two heads, and four arms. I thought he would be useful in a book, so I put him in. And then the trouble began. I called these consolidated twins Angelo and Luigi, and I tried to make them nice and agreeable, but it was not possible. They would not do anything my way, but only their own. They were wholly unmanageable, and not a day went by that they didn't develop some new kind of devilishness—particularly Luigi. Angelo was of a religious turn of mind, and was monotonously honest and honorable and upright, and tediously proper; whereas Luigi had no principles, no morals, no religion—a perfect blatherskite, and an inextricable tangle theologically—infidel, atheist, and agnostic, all mixed together. He was of a malicious disposition, and liked to eat things which disagreed with his brother. . . .

On the other hand, Angelo was a trouble to Luigi, the infidel, because he was always changing his religion, trying to find the best one, and he always preferred sects that believed in baptism by immersion, and this was a constant peril and discomfort to Luigi, who couldn't stand water outside or in; and so every time Angelo got baptized Luigi got drowned and had to be pumped out and resuscitated. Luigi was irascible, yet was never willing to stand by the consequences of his acts. He was always kicking somebody and then laying it on Angelo. And when the kicked person kicked back, Luigi would say, ''What are you kicking me for? I haven't done anything to you.'' Then the man would be sorry, and say, ''Well, I didn't mean any harm. I thought it was you; but, you see, you people have only one body between you, and I can't tell which of you I'm kicking. I don't know how to discriminate. I do not wish to be unfair, and so there is no way for me to do but kick one of you and apologize to the other.'' They were a troublesome pair in every way. If they did any work for you, they charged for two; but at the boarding house they ate and slept for two and only paid for one.

In the trains they wouldn't pay for two, because they only occupied one seat. The same at the theater. Luigi bought one ticket and deadheaded Angelo in. They couldn't put Angelo out because they couldn't put the deadhead out without putting out the twin that had paid, and scooping in a suit for damages.

Luigi grew steadily more and more wicked, and I saw by and by that the way he was going on he was certain to land in the eternal tropics, and at bottom I was glad of it; but I knew he would necessarily take his righteous brother down there with him, and that would not be fair. I did not object to it, but I didn't want to be responsible for it. I was in such a hobble that there was only one way out. To save the righteous brother I had to pull the consolidated twins apart and make two separate and distinct twins of them. Well, as soon as I did that, they lost all their energy and took no further interest in life. They were wholly futile and useless in the book, they became mere shadows, and so they remain. Mr. Mayo manages them, but if he had taken a chance at them before I pulled them apart and tamed them, he would have found out early that if he put them in his play they would take full possession and there wouldn't be any room in it for Pudd'nhead Wilson or anybody else.

I have taken four days to prepare these statistics, and as far as they go you can depend upon their being strictly true. I have not told all the truth about the twins, but just barely enough of it for business purposes, for my motto is—and Pudd'nhead Wilson can adopt it if he wants to—my motto is, "Truth is the most valuable thing we have; let us economize it" (Fatout, 1976, pp. 276-78).

Although no other writer has shown as much interest in conjoined twins as Mark Twain, there have been recurring expressions of fascination with their lives. These expressions, however, have followed the same theme that Twain pursued in relation to the lives of Siamese twins. As Robert Rowlette (1971) has pointed out, Twain's narratives on conjoined twins turned on their antagonistic natures. Behind the humor is the persistent question of how two such persons could hold different identities.

The celebrated novelist, Vladimir Nabokov, took an interest in conjoined twins in the 1950s. In a short story entitled "Scenes From the Life of a Double Monster," he explored both the perception of such people as freaks and the exploitation of their condition. In describing the reaction of the mother of his twins at birth he asks why being conjoined results in dehumanization.

I am not saying that a mother cannot love such a double thing—and forget in this love the dark dews of its unhallowed origin; I only think that the mixture of revulsion, pity, and a mother's love was too much for her. Both components of the double series before her staring eyes were healthy, handsome little components, with a silky fair fuzz on their violet-pink skulls, and well-formed rubbery arms and legs that moved like the many limbs of some wonderful sea animal. Each was eminently normal, but together they formed a monster. Indeed, it is strange to think that the presence of a mere band of tissue, a flap of flesh not much longer than a lamb's liver, should be able to transform joy, pride, tenderness, adoration, gratitude to God into horror and despair (1958, p. 167).

Nabokov's tale of the twins is one of a kidnapping. His conjoined twins are stolen from their village home for financial gain through exhibitions. In his narration one of the twins laments the loss of a time when "special" people were seen as having value beyond their worth for monetary purposes.

> If at that moment some adventurous stranger had stepped onto the shore from his boat in the bay, he would have surely experienced a thrill of ancient enchantment to find himself confronted by a gentle mythological monster in a landscape of cypresses and white stones. He would have worshiped it, he would have shed tears. But, alas, there was nobody to greet us there save that worried crook, our nervous kidnaper, a small doll-faced man wearing cheap spectacles, one glass of which was doctored with a bit of tape (p. 175).

Judith Rossner's novel *Attachments* is a story about two women who marry conjoined twins in the 1970s. A strong component of their attraction to the men is obviously their unusual condition. The book is filled with intimate details of their relationships. Rossner also emphasizes the marked differences in personality, tastes, and habits between the brothers. After several years of marriage and living with the realities of their special circumstance, the women convince the twins to undergo surgical separation. Following the surgery the differences in the brothers are reversed. This disrupts their marital and family lives, and results in the eventual dissolution of the relationships (Rossner, 1977).

A short story by John Barth goes beyond a portrayal of dissimilarities between conjoined twins to depict extreme antagonisms between his two characters. In "Petition," one of the brothers is writing an appeal for surgical separation. His plea is based on the irreconcilable differences he has with his twin. In his case he is joined at his abdomen to his brother's back by a short length of flesh. He is thus constantly looking over his twin's shoulder and is carried about in a piggyback fashion. In describing his misery he explains:

> We are nothing alike. I am slight, my brother is gross. He's incoherent but vocal; I'm articulate and mute. He's ignorant but full of guile; I think I may call myself reasonably educated, and if ingenuous, no more so I hope than the run of scholars. My

brother is gregarious: he deals with the public; earns and spends our income; tends (but slovenly) the house and grounds; makes, entertains, and loses friends; indulges in hobbies; pursues ambitions and women. For my part, I am by nature withdrawn, even solitary; an observer of life, a meditator, a taker of notes, a dreamer if you will—yet not a brooder; it's he who moods and broods, today hilarious, tomorrow despondent; I myself am stoical, detached as it were—of necessity, or I'd have long since perished of despair . . . I affirm our difference—all the difference in the world! . . . We have nothing in common but the womb that bore, the flesh that shackles, the grave that must soon receive us (Barth, 1969, pp. 59-60).

The fact that writers of fiction have chosen to focus on differences in conjoined twins is interesting. The manner in which they have presented these differences makes a survey and sampling of their works fascinating. Even more intriguing, however, is the evidence of actual differences which is to be found in accounts of their lives. This evidence will constitute the next chapter.

REFERENCES

Barth, J. (1969). *Lost in the funhouse.* New York: Bantam Books.

Fatout, P. (Ed.). (1976). *Mark Twain speaking.* Iowa City: University of Iowa Press.

Nabokov, V. (1958). *Nabokov's Dozen.* Garden City, NY: Doubleday.

Rossner, J. (1977). *Attachments.* New York: Simon and Schuster.

Rowlette, R. (1971). *Mark Twain's Pudd'nhead Wilson.* Bowling Green, OH: Bowling Green University Popular Press.

Twain, M. (1896). Personal habits of the Siamese twins. In *Sketches new and old.* New York: Macmillan.

_____. (1893). *Those extraordinary twins.* New York: Century Company.

Wiggins, R. (1951). Original of Mark Twain's 'Those extraordinary twins.' *American Literature, 23,* 355-57.

Six

Together But Different

As I was doing the research for this book I was surprised and pleased to find that over the years there have been several people who have been intrigued by the differences between conjoined twins and the nature/nurture issue. The earliest reference to this is in a book published in 1831 by Edward Lytton, entitled *The Siamese Twins: A Satirical Tale of the Times with Other Poems.* Although Eng's name is changed in the poem, it was obviously inspired by Chang and Eng, and must have been written shortly after their first exhibitions in America. Lytton opens the poem by referring to the philosophical challenge the lives of the twins created.

> I think, my own beloved Helvetius,
> Your reasoning was less sound than specious
> When you averred, howe'er the frame
> Varied—all minds were made the same
> That every colouring or gradation
> Was but the effect of education
> And rear'd alike, there had been no
> Difference 'twixt David Hume and Joe!
>
> I think tis clear, my Twins, who ne'er
> A moment could be separated,

Must almost every influence share
That e'er to either might be fated;
And little to the one or other
Could happen, nor affect the brother.

And yet they were as much dissimilar
As ever Honesty and Miller are;
For me, I have the Spurzheim mania,
And trace the mystery to their crania.

Now on—but first—a serious thing
To choose—upon their names we waver
Tis done' the gayer's Master Ching—
And Master Chang shall be the graver.

The poem continues for 252 pages. It explores the lives of the Siamese twins and draws lessons on human nature from their differences.

A few words concerning Lytton's references to Helvetius and Spurzheim are in order. Helvetius was a French writer and philosopher who lived in the eighteenth century. His writings helped shape the philosophical school of thought which came to be known as utilitarianism. Helvetius believed that all of a person's mental faculties are simply a form of sensation. He conceived of human nature as essentially passive and subject to manipulation. He argued that human development depends exclusively upon the environment and that there is no free will in human existence. Spurzheim was an Austrian physiologist. While studying medicine in Vienna, he was influenced by Franz Joseph Gall, the originator of phrenology. Spurzheim later became the most influential proponent of this doctrine. Phrenologists held that personality traits were determined by the size, shape, and contours of the brain. They believed that personalities could be "read" and behavior predicted by studying the characteristics of a person's skull. Phrenology, then, held that human development is determined by the innate physiology of the individual. Thus we see in the opening lives of Lytton's poem the portrayal of the environment/heredity debate which still resides with us today.

In 1841 as report was published in *The Proceedings of the American Philosophical Society* concerning an early attempt to study the psychological differences between Chang and Eng. The report was based on a paper that had actually been written in 1836. The author of the paper is referred to simply as Professor Tucker. In the paper entitled "Psychological Observations on the Siamese Twins, Cheng [sic] and Eng, Made in 1836," Professor Tucker explains his interest in the twins.

> Soon after the arrival of the Siamese twins into the United States, now above eleven years ago, it appeared to me . . . that they afforded an opportunity of making some psychological observations which had never before been presented, unless perchance by some like freak of nature.
> Here were two individuals who were precisely similar in all the circumstances likely to influence either their bodies or minds. They had always breathed the same air, eaten of the same food at the same time, slept and waked together, and taken the same exercises both in kind and quantity, and at the same moment. Whatever had affected the senses of the one, had affected those of the other. Their sources of knowledge, whether from observation or reasoning, and their lessons both of experience and education, were precisely the same. They had also been sick and well together, and may be supposed to have had in all respects, the same pleasures and pains, bodily and mental.
> Placed in circumstances so similar, or rather identical, these twins suggested the inquiry whether there was a correspondent resemblance in their faculties, passions and propensities; or if there was a diversity what was its nature and extent; and the result of the investigation seemed likely to shed no little light on the several theories, which have been put forth to explain the diversities of genius and mental character.
> It is known that some maintain with Helvetius, that these diversities among men whose organs have the ordinary degree of soundness, are the result of the particular circumstances in which the different individuals chance to be placed, while others insist that the cause of such diversities is to be attributed mainly to a difference of organization. Of this opinion was Dr. Gall, who further maintained that the mental faculties and propensities of each individual were indicated by small protuberances at the surface of the brain, and that these might be discovered by means of correspondent protuberances on the skull. There is a third class comprehending a much larger number both of vulgar and philo-

sophic minds, who think that our intellectual character depends partly on nature and partly on cultivation.

Now, if it should be found, on a careful comparison of the two brothers, that notwithstanding they had been placed in precisely similar circumstances, there was a marked difference in their faculties and tastes, they would seem to afford a satisfactory refutation of the doctrine of Helvetius. Should, however, no difference be discovered in their mental powers and propensities, then indeed, we should not be able to decide whether this close resemblance was to be attributed to the identity of circumstances in which they had been placed, or to that similarity of organization which is often seen in twins, and which nothing since their birth could, in this case, have disturbed (Psychological Observations, 1841, pp. 22-23).

In explaining his methodology Professor Tucker reveals what would be considered today to be flawed and naive techniques. Given the time and the circumstances, however, he probably used the best approach available to him. In order to examine possible differences in tastes and faculties in the twins the same questions were presented independently to Chang and Eng. The questions were whispered to Chang by Professor Tucker and to Eng by an assistant. The twins were instructed to whisper their responses to the examiners. The report includes a transcript of the questions and answers. Chang's name is spelled incorrectly throughout the report.

Question 1. What part of America puts you most in mind of Siam?
> Cheng. New Orleans.
> Eng. Louisiana.

2. Where did you stay longest in England?
> Both. In Glasgow.

3. Whom did you see first in London?
> Cheng. I did not know him.
> Eng. Charles something, but I can't recollect the whole name.

4. Have you been sick in this country? How long ill?
> Chang. Yes, twice, once fourteen days.

Eng. Yes, in New York, with a head-ache, and in Ohio with fever and ague.

By way of comparing their associating faculties, several words were then mentioned to them, and they were asked what these words suggested to their minds. Thus,

5. What does the word London suggest?
    Cheng. What a dark place it is. They went about in the day by torch-light.
    Eng. St. Paul's.

6. What, Liverpool, Boston?
    Cheng. Boston much the handsomest city.
    Eng. Liverpool is much the dirtiest.

7. What, manufactures?
    Cheng. The manufactures in Leeds.
    Eng. They suggest the idea of the ingenuity of man.

8. What, war?
    Cheng. The battle of New Orleans.
    Eng. Very bad article to deal with: I think folks could get along better without it.

9. What, money?
    Cheng. A mighty good thing.
    Eng. Very good I think—quite opposite to war.

10. Whom of all our great men do you most admire?
    Cheng. General Washington, John C. Calhoun.
    Eng. John C. Calhoun.

11. How large does the sun appear to you?
    Cheng. As big as this room.
    Eng. Not bigger than a decent sized centre table.

12. Are you willing to settle in America?
    Cheng. I think not.
    Eng. No.

13. What do you regard as the most useful invention?
    Cheng. A ship.
    Eng. Ship building.

14. What kind of animal food do you like best?
    Cheng. Ducks, geese and roast beef.
    Eng. Big goose.

15. What kind of vegetable food?
    Cheng. No particular preference.
    Eng. No choice—not being partial to any.

16. What kind of fruit?
    Cheng. Peaches, pears, melons.
    Eng. Musk melons.

17. What kind of perfume?
    Both. Rose.

18. What colour do you like best?
    Cheng. That depends upon what the thing is.
    Eng. That depends upon whether for coach, person, handkerchief, or coat.

19. What colour do you like best in flowers?
    There was a large vase in the room filled with flowers in great variety, and they both pointed to those that were of a saffron colour.

20. What season of the year do you prefer?
    Cheng. The spring.
    Eng. The fall of the year.

21. What kind of music do you like best?
    Both. The piano—the hunter's chorus.

22. What objects do you consider the handsomest, as possessing the greatest beauty?
    Cheng. I could not answer that: I see so many.
    Eng. Handsome women (ibid., pp. 24-26).

Professor Tucker makes a cautious interpretation of the results of his examination. He is quick to acknowledge the weaknesses and limitations of his observations. Combining his findings with information from their exhibition manager, however, he does make the following comments.

The greater energy of will and of purpose, which has been supposed [of Chang], may not exist, or if it does, it may be balanced by the greater powers of reflection possessed by Eng. Though the questions here propounded are too few to warrant any confident conclusions, we cannot but perceive that nearly half of his answers exhibit somewhat more of thought, or of precision than the

answers of his brother. If this be a just inference, it affords per-
suasive evidence against the theory of Helvetius. How far these
twins may support or refute the principles of phrenology, I did
not inquire; not only because an examination of their heads,
before their mental characters were accurately compared, would
be premature, but also because it would be more satisfactory if
made by those whose minds are more undecided about the merits
of Gall's system than mine can pretend to be (ibid., p. 27).

In conclusion Professor Tucker remarks that his report was written
not so much to give an account of the success of his experiment as to
stimulate interest in some reader in repeating it under more favorable
circumstances.

Such a one would have the advantage of the greater strength
which the peculiarities of these twins may be supposed to have
received from time and indulgence: he might propound to them a
greater number of questions, prepared with more care; he might
compare not merely a part of their mental faculties and propensities, but all of them; and lastly, he might ascertain whether the
further development and growth of their passions have cast a
shade over the interesting moral picture they once presented
(ibid., pp. 27-28).

A more comprehensive account of the difference between Chang and
Eng is contained in the description of their lives written by Judge
Graves. As discussed earlier, he knew the twins well and wrote down
his observations after their deaths.

Perhaps it may not be out of place here to give my recollection of
the men and their habits. They were men of as distinct mental individuality as any two brothers. In manner they were easy and
self poised and could be very agreeable when they wished; and
they were always desirous to make themselves agreeable to their
friends. In intellect, they were rather above the average of men.
Their perceptive faculties were very quick, much more than ordi-
narily so. The powers of memory were very great, especially of
duty, faces, money and locations. Both of them were men of far
more than ordinary memory. I have seen very few who surpassed

Eng. Although they usually came to correct conclusions their capacity for reasoning was not very great. In morality, they were honest, truthful, virtuous and sincere. If they pretended friendship you might know it was true; if they disliked one they had nothing to do with him. They were kind to their families and servants and particularly affectionate to each other. They were quick to resent insult, Chang having always being the most irritable. On a whole they were very good citizens, excellent neighbors and good friends. They were very fond of reading poetry and romances. Pope was their favorite author but they read Shakespeare, Byron, Kirkwhite and Fleetwood's "Life of Christ" with very great interest. Eng was the greatest reader of the two. He often read aloud to his brother and not infrequently to his family. He had partiality for Pope's poems. So great was Eng's partiality for Pope's poems, that he engaged in reading them the 10th time.

Although they had always each had his own individuality, each his own desires, passions, wishes and thoughts yet having always been subjected to the identically same influences their conclusion and sentiments, except in choosing their wives, had usually concurred. But after the partition of their property and the consequent diversity of interest different influences began to operate or rather the same influences operating on the mind of each produced very different result so that occasionally disagreements arose between the brothers but not half so frequently as between many not having such diversity of interest. In fact on one occasion their disagreement became so violent that under the excitement of the moment they actually fought each other (Graves, n.d., pp. 21-23).

When Dr. John C. Warren of the Harvard Medical School examined Chang and Eng he also noted that there were apparent differences between the two.

They differ in intellectual vigor. The perceptions of one are more acute than those of the other; and there is a corresponding coincidence in moral qualities. He who appears most intelligent, is somewhat irritable in temper; while the disposition of the other is extremely mild (Warren, 1829, p. 214).

Time after time in the records that exist of people who knew the Bunker twins or who examined them there are comments concerning their marked differences. They were clearly distinct individuals. Mark Twain's characterizations of one of the twins as a heavy drinker and one as a teetotaler was apparently grounded in fact.

In 1962 an article on the Bunker twins written by Jonathan Daniels, editor of Raleigh, North Carolina's *News and Observer,* was published in *American Heritage* magazine. Daniels shared an interest in the twins with his brother, Worth Daniels, a physician who had presented a paper on their deaths and autopsies to the American Clinical and Climatological Association. Jonathan Daniels's papers are housed in the Southern Historical Collection at the University of North Carolina. Included in that collection is a copy of a letter which was sent to his brother Worth by a researcher interested in the etiology of alcoholism. In the letter he explains his interest in Chang and Eng relative to alcoholism. The letter is difficult to follow in places but illustrates that the difference in the drinking habits of the twins had stimulated the writer to view them as a potential source of insight into the question of the origins of alcoholism.

Since they obviously MUST have had identical inheritant factors and to the greatest conceivable extent, identical environment, Chang's fairly well established alcoholism vs. Eng's lack of it certainly tends to support a physiological difference, regardless of whether Chang's drinking problem was acquired or inherent. I realize that the same argument could be applied to the condition if wholly mental, though not quite so forcibly.

At any rate I would like to know more about these twins and to that end, have written to the Chief of Police at White Plains, N.C., to ascertain whether any descendants of these twins are available—with two thoughts in mind; first to obtain as much information as exists about Chang and Eng and second, to learn if there had been any appreciable incidence of alcoholism among them.

This letter may prove to be a wild-goose chase since there is no real evidence of heredity transmission (especially on the male side). On the other hand, with such a large group it is likely that there has been some alcoholism among the first and subsequent generations. If this proves to be equally distributed (as is probable) between both branches, it would tend to negatively confirm the non-hereditary aspect, though not conclusively (Greenwood, 1962, p. 1).

If, as all available sources indicate, Eng was a complete abstainer then Chang must have been, indeed, a prodigious drinker. Contained in their papers in the Southern Historical Collection is a bill from a hotel where they stayed in May and June of 1870. The bill includes the following examples of alcoholic beverages which had been charged to the twins' account.

May 30
    Five bottles beer
    Two bottles wine
    One bottle whiskey

May 31
    Six bottles beer
    Two and half bottles wine
    One flask cognac

June 1
    Two bottles wine
    Eight bottles beer
    One flask cognac
    One bottle whiskey

At the time that observations were made of the traits and temperaments of Chang and Eng the science of psychology was in its infancy. The information available concerning them is rich but it is limited according to contemporary standards of psychological assessment. This is true of all of the earliest records of conjoined twins. In 1911, for example, the *British Medical Journal* published an article entitled ''A Problem of Personality.'' It concerned Rosa and Josepha Blazek and described their differences in preferences for food and drink. One liked beer, the other preferred wine. One was partial to salad, the other disliked it. They had different patterns of sleeping and waking, and their pulses differed. Along with a few other physiological measurements, this was the extent of the ''psychological'' data offered in the article.

Later in this century, however, reports began to be published about conjoined twins which contained the kind of information which is more typical of the contents of psychological evaluations today. In 1948 a case study of Mary and Margaret Gibb was published in the *Journal of the American Medical Association.* (The lives of Mary and Margaret, like Rosa and Josepha and most of the other twins discussed in the remainder of this chapter, are described in Chapter 4.) At the age of thirty-four Margaret was described as thin, high-strung, and apprehensive, while Mary was characterized as stout, calm, and placid. Their mother stated that her daughters had always been different; Margaret had consistently been concerned about her health and financial state while Mary was easygoing and apparently carefree. On the Otis Intelligence Test they received similar scores (both had intelligence quotients of approximately 80). On the Minnesota Multiphasic Personality Inventory, however, her responses showed Margaret to be higher than average in the hypochondriac, depressive, and hysteria scales. Mary was within normal range on all scales of the inventory. On the Rorschach ink blots Margaret showed indications of manifest anxiety. The article suggests that Margaret's chronic anxiety and nervous tension were causal factors in her high blood pressure (Jones et al., 1948).

The conjoined twins most studied by psychologists were Violet and Daisy Hilton. In 1927 Helen Koch reported the results of her extensive psychological testing of the twins in the *Journal of Comparative Psychology.* Koch explained her interest in examining the twins in the opening paragraph of the article.

> The extent to which Siamese twins differ from each other rather than the manner of their similarity is, from one point of view, the focus of interest as far as the bearing of the phenomenon on the problem of hereditary versus environmental influences is concerned. These individuals represent, presumably a case of identical heredity and as nearly an identical environment as is possible in human beings . . . (Koch, 1927, p. 313).

Daisy and Violet were fourteen years old when the examinations were conducted. After describing the physical characteristics of the girls, Koch commented on their educational backgrounds. The twins had apparently had a series of tutors from the time they were seven years old. Those aspects of education which would increase their abilities as performers in traveling shows and on the vaudeville circuit were emphasized. Music was one such focus. The girls played the saxophone, clarinet, and piano. The twins could sew and they told Koch that they enjoyed reading, especially detective stories. Daisy and Violet also told her that they shared most of the same interests.

Daisy and Violet were given several tests of intelligence and scholastic abilities. Daisy's performance on these tests was consistently superior to Violet's. In tests that involved reading skills Daisy also surpassed Violet. Koch reported that Daisy read more painstakingly than her sister and was better able, in general, to reproduce more of what she saw and heard. She said that these differences in reading skills were "large and rather significant" (ibid., p. 325).

A word association test elicited very different reactions from the girls. Violet gave many more unusual associations to the stimulus words presented to her than Daisy. Most interesting, however, was the fact that out of the list of 100 words the girls responded with the same association in only eight instances.

A high degree of dissimilarity characterized the twins in their reactions to a test of "emotional attitudes." Violet's responses were interpreted as being indicative of a greater number of "worries, of pleasures, and activities believed to be wicked" (ibid., p. 331). According to comparisons of the twins' responses to the test to established norms, Koch reported that Daisy was considerably more mature in her emotional attitudes than Violet.

Koch was cautious in her interpretation of the test results she presented in the article. Repeatedly she questioned the magnitude and significance of the differences she found between Daisy and Violet. To her credit, she also questioned the tests themselves as valid measures of these differences and the meaning of these differences when compared to the performance of other samples (for example, identical, nonconjoined twins). At least one reader (Hirsch, 1930) placed more confidence in her results than she expressed. Koch was also concerned about the fact that each conjoined twin becomes a part of the environment of the other, thus making their environments for development, from that perspective, different. Suffice it to say that Koch approached the results of her research prudently if not tentatively.

Although Koch's article was published in 1927 she had actually examined the fourteen-year-old Hilton twins in 1922. In 1932, when Daisy and Violet were twenty-four years old, they were observed for

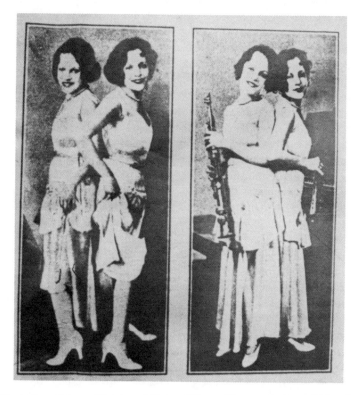

Illustration 6.1. Violet and Daisy Hilton. Photograph from "The Self-expression of Identical Twins in Handwriting and Drawing," by E. Seeman and R. Saudek, 1932, *Character and Personality, 1*, p. 114.

psychological differences by Ernest Seeman and Robert Saudek. In giving some background information on the twins Seeman and Saudek quote a friend who had long known them intimately.

In literature and in drama, Daisy likes romanticism. She likes to be carried away by the imaginative adventure stories of Conrad and Sabatini. She likes the sentimentality of J. M. Barrie. She likes the phantom world of airy, gossamer things that lie behind the twinkling stars and twilight of early evening, whose ghosts steal in and out through the shadows. Violet doesn't like romanticism at all—her interest is in the reality of things, in attaining a philosophical understanding of life. She likes to pit her young mind against the unsolved mysteries of time. And in that questioning and curiosity, there is something that satisfies Daisy. Both are "home" girls—and proud of their ability to perform household duties. Daisy sews. She delights in designing and making delicate little pieces of needlecraft. Violet is not particularly fond of sewing; rather, she likes to concern herself with the arrangement of things—furniture, bric-a-brac, pictures. Violet likes to cook. Her skill in culinary art is very diversified and genuine. But carrying out their usual rule of cheerful compromise, Daisy helps Violet cook, although she doesn't enjoy it to any great extent and would rather sew. But Violet also helps Daisy at her sewing (Seeman and Saudek, 1932, p. 115).

Seeman and Saudek then interject a disclaimer of the identical nature of the environmental influences in the twins' development. It is similar to the statement made by Koch in her article. Both of these statements will be discussed at the end of this chapter.

An environment more similar than these twins have lived under every hour of their lives could hardly be conceived, and yet it has not been altogether identical. For though so identical physically as to be nourished by the same blood-stream, there have been subtle differences in the daily impingements of, and reactions to, external stimuli. Each sister has had her own private experiences. Daisy may have written a letter while Violet dined; or Violet may have contemplated the landscape from the car window while Daisy was chatting with a fellow-traveler. One frequently sleeps while the other reads a book. And no less individual than their waking thoughts, the dreams of each are entirely separate and distinct (ibid., p. 116).

Seeman and Saudek used only two techniques for investigating the similarities and differences in the personalities of Violet and Daisy. They asked each of the twins to draw a house, a tree, and a person (this test, known as the H-T-P, is a common form of personality assessment), and they took handwriting samples. On the basis of these measures they concluded that Daisy and Violet were very similar in personality attributes. Concerning the twins' drawings they said that "The draw-ings are as similar in conception and technique as if they were done by the same person" (ibid.). I find their observation most difficult to understand or accept. Illustration 6.2 is a reproduction of the drawings done by Violet and Daisy. To me the differences in the pictures are striking.

Seeman and Saudek also found the handwriting styles of Violet and Daisy to be almost identical. Illustrations 6.3 and 6.4 are the samples included in the article. I claim absolutely no understanding of hand-writing analysis. I leave it to you, the reader, to determine how similar the styles appear to be.

In summarizing their finding the authors make several statements that appear to me to be rather confusing.

> There are hardly any dissimilarities, because we can account for all apparently variant features by considering the ambidexterity of both twins, by the fact that Violet happened to write with her right, and Daisy with her left hand, and that Violet has attained a somewhat greater fluency in the routine of writing.
>
> To us it is rather remarkable that Prof. Newman [H. H. New-man devoted considerable research to the study of identical twins and had seen the Hilton twins. He is referred to later in this chapter.] was struck by the dissimilarities rather than the similari-ties of these twins, because, judging from their drawings and writings only, as we are now doing, they appear the most similar pair [several pairs of identical twins were presented in the article] that we have come across so far (ibid., p. 121).

In 1964 Sidney Cleveland and his colleagues reported on their psy-chological appraisal of a pair of conjoined twins. The twins were passing through Houston, Texas, with a traveling circus and agreed to be examined by the authors of the report at Baylor Medical School. The male twins were twelve years old at the time of the examination. Their names were not disclosed in the report and they do not fit the descrip-tion of any of the other twins that have been previously discussed. In explaining their interest in examining the boys, Cleveland and his coauthors present a perspective that is somewhat different from the other cases we have reviewed.

Illustration 6.2.   Drawings by Daisy and Violet Hilton, from "The Self-expression of Identical Twins in Handwriting and Drawing," by E. Seeman and R. Saudek, 1932, *Character and Personality, 1,* p. 116.

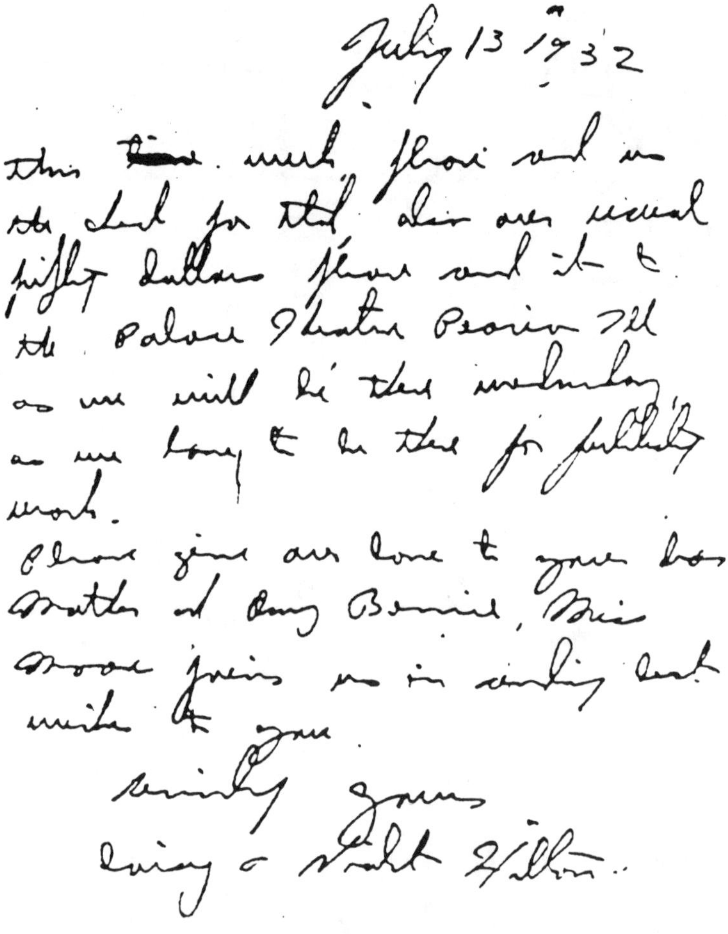

Illustration 6.3.   Sample of Daisy Hilton's handwriting, from "The Self-expression of Identical Twins in Handwriting and Drawing," by E. Seeman and R. Saudek, 1932, *Character and Personality, 1,* p. 118.

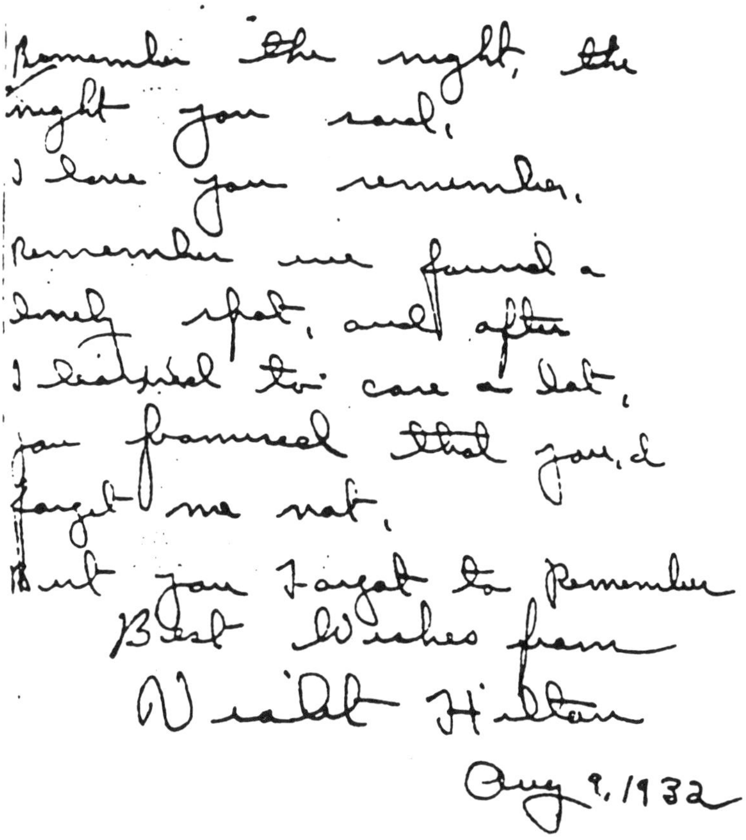
Remember the night, the
night you said,
I love you remember.
Remember we found a
lonely spot, and after
I learned to care a lot,
you promised that you'd
forget me not,
But you forgot to Remember
Best Wishes from
Violet Hilton
Aug 9, 1932

Illustration 6.4. Sample of Violet Hilton's handwriting, from "The Self-expression of Identical Twins in Handwriting and Drawing," by E. Seeman and R. Saudek, 1932, *Character and Personality, 1,* p. 119.

The examination of conjoined twins is of scientific interest and value for a variety of reasons. For one thing, such twins are of interest in their own rights as presenting a rare and unfortunate human condition. Moreover, study of inseparably linked twins also yields information on the techniques employed by individuals in adjusting to a frustrating and doomed life situation. Careful study of united twins has already suggested that despite the sharing of identical hereditary and environmental backgrounds, as individuals each twin member struggles to evolve a degree of uniqueness as a separate identity (Cleveland et al., 1964, p. 266).

The twins were given the Peabody Picture Vocabulary Test (Form A to one, Form B to the other) as a measure of intellectual functioning. One achieved a mental age of eleven years, nine months for an IQ equivalent of 99. The other scored a mental age of ten years, two months for an IQ equivalent of 87. This twelve-point difference in IQ appears to be a rather marked dissimilarity in performance for the two boys. Interpretation of this finding, however, must be tempered with the question of the reliability in using two different forms of the test. The questionable validity of IQ comparisons in general must also be considered.

The twins were further tested using ink blot tests, drawing samples, and other measures which were intended to yield a picture of the overall personalities of the brothers rather than the more confined question of intelligence as assessed with the Peabody. The picture drawn by Cleveland and his associates from these assessments is rather tragic. The boys are portrayed as being obsessed with their condition and struggling hopelessly to find a way to be free of each other. Their findings led then to a rather somber but interesting conclusion.

It would appear that a paradox has been created; conjoined twins show certain personality differences yet they share a fused identity. How can this apparent paradox be resolved? Normal twins have at their disposal a variety of roles to be played in a variety of situations. Conjoined twins are always required to act out their roles in the same situation. They are permitted no variety or separation of social or physical situations. The stage setting for their role playing never varies. Within the narrow confines permitted them, conjoined twins work out a superficially contrasting but fixed set of roles, usually complementing each other's be-havior. Thus, the literature on conjoined twins reveals that when-ever personality differences are described, they fall into contrast-ing categories. If one twin is aggressive, the other is passive; if one likes sweets, the other prefers sour tastes; if one is resistive, the other is tractable. These apparent opposites in behavior may be viewed as attempts to create a verified behavioral model, to encompass within a single organism a range of activity. Like bookends, conjoined twins' remain fixed at opposing ends of a single continuum (ibid., pp. 269-70).

The concept of a continuum has importance in attempting to under-stand the lives of conjoined twins but perhaps not in the way that Cleve-land and his collaborators presented it. In a 1982 essay entitled "Living with Connections," Stephen Jay Gould explored the idea of whether conjoined twins are two distinct individuals. He was stimulated to pursue this question when in a Paris museum he discovered the skele-tons of Rita and Christina, a pair of nineteenth-century conjoined infants who were born in Sardinia. He was further inspired when he found a copy of a voluminous account of the autopsy and explanation of their condition which followed their deaths at five months of age.

Gould discusses the fact that a fertilized human egg normally devel-ops into a single individual but that on rare occasions following concep-tion, the dividing cells separate into two discrete groups. This, of course, results in what we call identical twins and they are genetic "carbon copies."

In some ultimate, biological sense, they are the same iterated individual—and the psychological literature contains ample testimony to feelings of imperfect separation shared by many so-called identical twins. Yet, at least for definition's sake, we have no difficulty in identifying one-egg human twins as undeniably separate personalities for two excellent reasons: first, physical separation is the essence of our vernacular definition of individ-uality; second, human personalities are so subtly and pervasively shaped by complex environments of life (whatever the quirky similarities between one-egg twins reared apart) that each person follows a unique path (Gould, 1982, p. 22).

Gould points out, however, that when the physical separation of one-egg twins is not complete we have greater difficulty in discerning the individuality of the twins. Difficulty in recognizing this continuum from single development of a fertilized egg, to identical twins, to conjoined twins has led to puzzlement and debate over the centuries. He believes it has resulted in the overriding question that has always surrounded the occurrence of conjoined twins, the question of individuality. Are conjoined twins one person or two?

One or two? This question indeed must be central to the popular interest, the sideshow fascination, which has always been drawn to conjoined twins. For those who have known such twins best or who have studied them most closely the answer, however, is clear. Each twin in a conjoined pair is a unique individual. Luigi Gedda, an Italian geneticist, and Lionel Penrose of University College in London, also a geneticist, reported that they found greater differences among conjoined twins than in ordinary identical twins (Gaddis and Gaddis, 1972). The scientist who concerned himself most with conjoined twins was Dr. H. H. Newman of the University of Chicago.

Horatio Newman, who was interested in twins in general, also observed that conjoined twins were more different than other identical twins. When he examined the Hilton sisters he found them to be less similar to each other than almost any separate identical twins he had known (Gaddis and Gaddis, 1972).

To explain these striking differences in conjoined twins Newman developed an interesting theory. He argued that at a certain stage of development, the embryonic cell mass begins to develop a right and a left side. These sides are like each other but rather than exact duplicates they are mirror images of each other. It is similar, he said, to the way in which your right hand is not a duplicate of your left but like its image in a mirror.

Newman reasoned that if the separation of the cell mass which results in identical twins takes place before this mirror imaging (asymmetry) develops then the resulting twins will be very much alike—almost exact duplicates of each other. If, however, the separation takes place after the mirror imaging of the cell mass is established, the twins will be opposites in many respects. One, for example, may be left-handed while the other is right-handed. The hair whorls and fingerprints of one twin may be the reverse of the other. If twinning comes too late to permit the complete separation of the two halves of the cell mass, Newman speculated, conjoined twins are formed that are complete reversals of each other (Newman, 1940).

Newman eventually came to believe that mirror imaging was due primarily to the differential influence of growth-depressing agents on the incompletely separated cell masses that result in conjoined twins. He felt that somehow the prenatal growth of one of the twins was slowed down and that this resulted in physical and mental differences in the twins in later development. In this sense he attributed the differences to an environmental influence, a dissimilarity in the uterine environment of the two twins. Upon reaching this conclusion he abandoned his "earlier view that mirror imaging is due to a 'third factor, neither strictly genetic nor environmental' " (Newman, 1940, p. 34).

Most people who have studied conjoined twins and observed their differences have, like Newman, striven to find the explanation for these differences in either genetics or the environment. Some early investigators argued that the twins must have begun as nonidentical, genetically different twins that were somehow fused during embryonic development. Others, as mentioned earlier in this chapter, have held that each twin, being part of the environment of the other, exerts a different influence and that this results in a different personality for each. This argument seems to overlook the fact that if each twin creates a different environment for the other, these differences themselves must have a genesis. To pursue this perspective is to engage in chicken-egg reasoning.

The evidence I have presented in this chapter on differences between conjoined twins "proves" nothing. It is essentially a collection of case studies gleaned from disparate sources. Each case could, and should, be viewed with a critical eye. Each could be dismissed because of its flaws or limitations. It is the sum of the cases that I find compelling. I have found it compelling enough to write this book. I have found it to be intriguing and disturbing enough to send me on the theoretical search which I describe in the final chapter. Before describing that search, however, it is important to place the significance of the data on conjoined twins within the context of research on twins in psychological literature.

REFERENCES

A problem of personality. (1911). *British Medical Journal*, June, 1397-98.

Cleveland, S., Reitman, E., & Sheer, D. (1964). Psychological appraisal of conjoined twins. *Journal of Projective Techniques, 28,* 265-70.

Daniels, J. (1962). Never alone at last. *American Heritage, 13,* 29-31, 106-8.

Gaddis, V., & Gaddis, M. (1972). *The curious world of twins.* New York: Hawthorn Books.

Gould, S. (1982). Living with connections. *Natural History, 91,* 18, 20, 22.

Graves, J. (n.d.). *Life of Eng and Chang Bunker, the original Siamese twins.* Surry County, NC: Surry County Historical Society.

Greenwood, R. (1962). Letter to Worth Daniel, Jonathan Daniels Collection, 3466, Box 104, Folder 8. Southern Historical Collection, University of North Carolina.

Hirsch, N. (1930). *Twins: Heredity and environment.* Cambridge: Harvard University Press.

Jones, S., Youngblood, O., & Evans, J. (1948). Human parabiotic pygopagus twins with hypertension. *Journal of the American Medical Association, 138,* 642-45.

Koch, H. (1927). Some measurements of a pair of siamese twins. *Journal of Comparative Psychology, 7,* 313, 333.

Lytton, E. (1831). *The Siamese twins: A satirical tale of the times with other poems.* New York: J. & J. Harper.

Newman, H. H. (1940). The question of mirror imaging in human one-egg twins. *Human Biology, 12,* 21-34.

Psychological observations of the Siamese twins. (1841). *Proceedings of the American Philosophical Society, 2,* 22-28.

Seeman, E., & Saudek, R. (1932). The self-expression of identical twins in handwriting and drawing. *Character and Personality, 1,* 91-128.

Warren, J. (1829). Account of the Siamese twin brothers. *American Journal of Science, 17,* 212-16.

Part Three

Arguments, Reflections, and Questions

Seven

Nature, Nurture, and Twins

In 1937 Horatio Newman and two of his associates at the University of Chicago published a study of identical twins who had been raised in separate environments. Included in the nineteen case studies in the book was the case of Ed and Fred. A few years earlier Ed, a telephone company service man, had been greeted in a familiar manner by a new man at work who addressed Ed as Fred. When the new worker learned that Ed was not the Fred that he knew, he found it hard to believe. When another man mistook Ed for Fred and explained that he looked just like an acquaintance in another city, Ed set out to find his "twin."

He found Fred and discovered that, indeed, they were identical twins. They had been separated through adoption by different families when they were six months old. The families were not acquainted and both Ed and Fred had been raised as only children. The families moved to different states and there was no contact until Ed and Fred reunited themselves as adults.

The twins found that they had much in common. Neither had been very good students and both were high school dropouts. Both had married and had a son; their sons were born around the same time. Both were employed by the telephone company. Incredibly, both had a dog named Trixie! When Newman and his associates tested Ed and Fred they found that their IQ scores were only one point apart.

Cases like Ed and Fred seem to emerge periodically and they capture the public's attention. People are fascinated by accounts of identical twins who were separated in infancy or early childhood and who marry women with the same first name, like the same brand of beer, or drive the same model of car. The public fascination with such incidents is reflective of a corresponding scientific fascination with cases of separated identical twins.

Research on the question of the inheritance of human traits has been largely focused on the similarities or differences in individuals from the same family. This kind of research has generally consisted of correlational studies of specific intellectual, physical, and personality characteristics in people who are somehow related. Human beings, however, may be related not only because they share common genes but also because they have experienced shared environments. Parents and their children may resemble each other more than persons who are unrelated to them both because they have many of the same genes *and* because of commonalities in home environment, socioeconomic status, education, the opportunities available to them, and a myriad of other nonhereditary variables. Because of this confounding reality in the nature/nurture question, scientists and philosophers have been drawn to those exceptions to the usual human experience which promise to help them exorcise the mystery of heredity versus environment.

One such exception is the occurrence of identical twins. Identical twins (who are by definition exact genetic duplicates) have posed the question of whether they are substantially similar to each other even when they have been separated at birth or early in life. Are they closely related in their characteristics even though they have experienced different environments?

A problem with this method of research is that it can only be considered valid if the assumption is made that the environments in which the separated identical twins were reared were different in significant ways. This problem has often been amazingly trivialized or even ignored. Research on the inheritance of intelligence in particular has been plagued by difficulties in design, sample size, and even by apparent fraudulence.

Sir Cyril Burt, a British psychologist, was an enthusiastic investigator of the concept of the genetic transmission of mental traits. He believed that low IQ and poor academic performance were the result of "inborn inferiority of general intelligence" (Chorover, 1979, p. 49).

Burt was best known for his studies of identical twins who were raised apart. His data indicated that even when these twins were raised in very different environments their IQs were strikingly similar. According to Burt, this provided evidence that it was the genetic inheritance of the twins, not the environment in which they were raised, which was the primary determinant of their intelligence.

In his book, *Genetics and Education,* Arthur Jensen, the most noted contemporary proponent of the genetic basis of intelligence, praises Burt as the most distinguished exponent of the overall study of the heritability of intelligence and says that Burt's writings are a "must" for all students of the psychology of individual differences. Jensen saved his greatest praise, however, for Burt's twin studies and reported on them extensively in his own work.

Following Cyril Burt's death, Professor Leon Kamin of Princeton University reviewed the data on Burt's twin studies. He noticed that, although the number of pairs of twins used in the several studies varied, the correlations Burt reported between the intelligence test scores of twins raised apart remained the same (see Table 7.1). The chances for

Table 7.1
Cyril Burt's Reported Correlations in the Twin Studies

Year of Report	Identical Twin Raised Apart	
	Number of Pairs	*Correlation*
1955	21	.771
1958	42	.771
1966	53	.771

Source: Adapted from Kamin, 1974, p. 38.

this kind of statistical consistency occurring in separate studies using different sample sizes is infinitesimal. Kamin looked more closely at Burt's work and found that this sort of statistical constancy was scattered throughout his research. Kamin finally came to the conclusion that Burt's work on the twins simply could not be accepted with any confidence as being scientifically valid. In 1976 a medical reporter for the London *Sunday Times* stated that he had found evidence that the assistants whom Burt had said worked with him on the twin studies never existed. Dr. Oliver Gillie, the reporter, said that the people who Burt claimed had seen the raw data in the studies, helped him perform the statistical analyses, and who he listed as coauthors of the reports either never existed or could not have been in contact with Burt when the work was done. In his biography of Cyril Burt, L. S. Hearnshaw corroborated the charge that Burt had doctored his findings in the twin studies and created mythical assistants. He also found other instances of fraud and distortion in Burt's work (Hearnshaw, 1979).

Cyril Burt's research aside, there are three other studies of separated identical twins that have served as the primary body of evidence in arguments for the hereditary nature of intelligence. One is the 1937 study by Newman and his colleagues that included Ed and Fred. A second was reported by Shields in 1962, and the third by Juel-Nielsen in 1965. As mentioned earlier, the Newman study involved nineteen pairs of American twins. The Shields research included fifty-three pairs of English twins and the Juel-Nielsen study consisted of descriptions of twelve pairs of Danish twins. In each case the correlations of IQ scores for the identical twins who had been raised in separate environments were quite high. The Newman study yielded a correlation of .67, the Shields finding was .77, and Juel-Nielsen reported a correlation of .62. These studies, along with Cyril Burt's data, have been cited repeatedly in the literature of those disciplines concerned with the sources of human characteristics. They have been presented as evidence of the dominant influence of genetics in determining intelligence. They have been described and quoted in textbooks, articles, and in mass distribution publications. These studies have thus made an impact on the thinking of generations of students and professionals.

The validity and potency of these studies of separated twins have been derived from several basic assumptions. Howard Taylor (1980) has pointed out that the strength of these studies is based on certain confidences that would lead readers to believe that environmental factors in their lives had been significantly separate and different so that any similarity in IQs of the twins could, indeed, be attributed to heredity. Among the requirements that Taylor delineated for placing confidence in this type of research are (1) that the twins were, in fact separated at birth; and (2) that they were raised after separation in different, unrelated families and in dissimilar social environments.

Taylor examined four sources of environmental similarity in the identical twins who have been used as subjects in the three separation studies. Each of these sources was, he feels, overlooked or not analyzed by the authors of the reports. The first is the factor of late separation. He found that the actual age of separation of twins in the studies varied and observed that the longer twins had been exposed to common family, educational and social environments the greater the correlation would be expected between twins due to those common influences.

A second variable that Taylor found was not addressed in the studies was reunion of the twins prior to IQ testing. He argues that the length of time that twins had been reunited should have been an important consideration in the studies but was not taken into account.

The third factor that, according to Taylor, could have influenced the results in all three studies was the relatedness of adoptive families. He found that in the vast majority of cases the twins had been placed in branches of the same family, in families of close friends, or in the same orphanage. A common situation was for one twin to be raised by its biological mother while the other was raised by a relative, such as an aunt, uncle, or grandparent. Obviously these twins shared more environmental similarities than twins raised in families actually unrelated.

The final factor that Taylor discusses is that of social similarity in the environments in which the twins were raised. He found that in some cases the twins were even raised in environments that allowed frequent contact between them. Some twins, for example, attended the same school. Some twins had adoptive parents with identical or similar occupations, education, or incomes. Some of the twins saw each other every day.

These confounding features of research on separated identical twins do raise serious questions about the confidence which can be placed in the reported results. A few specific examples will make this even more evident. Lewontin, Rose, and Kamin provide such examples in their discussion of the studies (1984).

Kenneth and Jerry, twin subjects in the Newman study, were adopted by different families. Both, however, had adoptive fathers who were firemen with limited educations. They had lived in the same city for two years. Harold and Holden, another Newman pair, had both been adopted by relatives. They lived only three miles apart and attended the same school.

In the Shields study Jessie and Winifred, who were separated at three months, were actually brought up within a few hundred yards of each other. After they discovered each other at school at the age of five, they were told they were twins. They played with each other a great deal; they were described as being together all the time. They wanted to share the same desk at school. Bertram and Christopher were adopted by paternal aunts who brought them up next door to each other. They were constantly in and out of each other's houses. Oddette and Fanny were separated only between the ages of three and eight. Even during that period they traded places every six months between their mother and their maternal grandmother. Benjamin and Ronald were brought up in the same village. Benjamin was raised by his mother, Ronald by his grandmother. They went to school together and continued to live in the same village as adults. They were fifty-two years old when they went to London to have their IQs tested by Shields. Joanna and Isabel were separated for the first five years of their lives. After that, however, they attended the same school. They were fifty years old when they were tested.

In the Juel-Nielsen study Ingregard and Monika were each cared for by a relative until the age of seven. They then lived together with their mother until the age of fourteen. The twins were described as dressing alike, being confused for each other at school (and even by their stepfather), and as playing only with each other.

Lewontin, Rose, and Kamin conclude their review of these examples by commenting on the obvious limitations that realities such as these would seemingly place on the validity of the studies. ''Remember that these and similar separated twin pairs are the bedrock upon which the scientific study of the heritability of IQ has been based. The ludicrous shortcomings of these studies are obvious to the most naive of nonscientific eyes. Perhaps only a scientist caught up with an enthusiasm for an abstract idea and trained to accept the 'objectivity' of numbers could take such studies seriously'' (Lewontin et al., 1984, p. 109).

There are many other instances of the use of twins (both identical and fraternal) in psychological and medical research. In many cases they have been studied in ways that inspire more confidence and have yielded more valuable results than in the studies we have discussed. I have focused on these because they illustrate the fascination that has been drawn to identical twins in the context of the nature/nurture debate and to reveal the weaknesses which have characterized that fascination.

We now return to conjoined twins. It is obvious that I am indeed "caught up with the enthusiasm of an abstract idea." I doubt, however, that I can be accused of having allowed my training to have led me "to accept the 'objectivity' of numbers." The data discussed on conjoined twins lack the neatness of numbers and are unorthodox by some scientific standards. Given its limitations, however, it led me to search for a place in the heredity/environment equation for human freedom.

REFERENCES

Chorover, S. (1979). *From genesis to genocide.* Cambridge, MA: MIT Press.

Hearnshaw, L. S. (1979). *Cyril Burt, psychologist.* London: Hodder and Stoughton.

Jensen, A. (1972). *Genetics and education.* New York: Harper and Row.

Juel-Nielsen, N. (1965). Individual and environment: A psychiatric and psychological investigation of monozygous twins raised apart. *Acta Psychiatrica et Neurologica Scandinavica,* Supplement 183.

Kamin, L. (1974). *The science and politics of IQ.* Potomac, MD: Lawrence Erlbaum Associates.

Lewontin, R., Rose, S., & Kamin, L. (1984). *Not in our genes.* New York: Pantheon Books.

Newman, H., Freeman, F., & Holzinger, K. (1937). *Twins: A study of heredity and environment.* Chicago: University of Chicago Press.

Shields, J. (1962). *Monozygotic twins brought up apart and brought up together.* London: Oxford University Press.

Taylor, H. (1980). *The IQ game: A methodological inquiry into the heredity-environment controversy.* New Brunswick, NJ: Rutgers University Press.

Eight

Heredity, Environment, and More

In an article on the role of values in science, George Howard paraphrased Mahatma Gandhi who wrote that there are seven sins in the world: wealth without work, pleasure without conscience, knowledge without character, commerce without morality, science without humanity, worship without sacrifice, and politics without principle. Howard speculates on what Gandhi meant by portraying science without humanity as a sin. He fears that for the science of psychology the legacy of being without humanity could mean that psychology runs the risk of having an impoverished vision of humanity. He warns that by viewing humans from an unduly restricted perspective, a paralyzing myopia may be perpetrated that results in diminishing rather than expanding the potential of individuals and of the human species as a whole. Howard believes that our challenge today is to construct a science built upon an image of humanity that acknowledges and values human nature in all of its diversity, complexity, and subtlety (Howard, 1985, p. 264).

Chang and Eng, and the other conjoined twins described in this book have served as a challenge to me to expand what for some time I had felt was my own restricted view of humanity. It was a view that I was uncomfortable with but had not actively sought to reconstruct for myself. The intriguing differences I discovered in these twins led me to search for ideas that would accommodate these differences and provide me with a more vital conception of human characteristics and behavior. In this chapter I will share the ideas I have found that allow me to begin to transcend that more narrow view of humanity and to begin to construct an image of human nature that is more "diverse, complex and subtle."

The idea that heredity and environment are the only factors that can possibly influence human development is ingrained not only within the scientific community but, more widely, in our culture. The concept that something else could influence the development of an individual is likely to be viewed as naive or even ludicrous. To explore the concept that there is a quality of freedom, choice, or intention in human life is also, however, to risk being accused of having violated the principles of science. Freedom is more likely to be viewed as a proper subject for philosophy, religion, or even mysticism than for science. That is one of the reasons that I was so drawn to the evidence of differences in conjoined twins. It is the only "data" of which I am aware that indicate that choice and self direction are a reality in the way people grow and live. At least this data should cause us to consider freedom as a potential variable in the human equation.

I have come to believe that it is not heredity and environment as a conceptionalization of human development that is the culprit. It is the manner in which we have viewed heredity and environment that reduces our view of humanity. Heredity not only creates our physiology, it creates a physiology which allows us to be creative and flexible individuals. The environment not only molds us but also offers us a continually changing spectrum of opportunities. I have come to believe that the flaw in our thinking is not that we have been taught to view ourselves as the products of heredity and environment alone. It is, rather, the ways in which we have come to view heredity and environment, reductionistically and deterministically.

Biological determinists (the genetic radicals on the nature/nurture question) reduce human beings to the sum of their genetic endowment. Environmental determinists (the "blank slate" extremists on this question) portray people as being nothing more than the product of the molding influences of the physical, familial, and cultural contexts in which they grow and exist.

The battle between biological and environmental determinism has raged for centuries. Philosophy, psychology, sociology, theology, and other disciplines have been occupied and preoccupied with this dispute in unproductive and, often, inflammatory ways. The traditional portrayal of the question has been "either—or"; either it is heredity that is responsible for what we become as human beings or it is the impact of the environment which causes the particular characteristics of a human life.

Many people have recognized the absurdity of both of these extremist views. Even a casual examination of the issue compels one to recognize that people are both biological and cultural creatures. Still, the extremism persists.

Perhaps the most recent and popularly received argument for the largely genetic determination of human behavior is that of E. O. Wilson. As the primary proponent of what has come to be known as sociobiology, Wilson has received much attention for his theory that most human behavior, including such attributes as altruism and religious belief, are at their core hereditary in origin. Wilson's approach then is primarily one of biological determinism. In the following quote, even though he alludes to interactions between heredity and environment, it is clear that Wilson finds no room in his theory for human freedom.

> The great paradox of determinism and free will, which has held the attention of the wisest philosophers and psychologists for generations, can be phrased in biological terms as follows: If our genes are inherited and our environment is a train of physical events set in motion before we were born, how can there be a truly independent agent within the brain? The agent itself is created by the interaction of the genes and the environment. It would appear that our freedom is only a self delusion (Wilson, 1978, p. 71).

Wilson then reformulates the question of human freedom by posing it as a question of predictability. For Wilson the line of reasoning under discussion is that people are unpredictable and, only in that sense, are they free.

> The mind is too complicated a structure, and human social relations effect its decision in too intricate and variable a manner, for the detailed histories of individual human beings to be predicted in advance by the individuals affected or by other human beings. You and I are consequently free and responsible persons in this fundamental sense'' (ibid., p. 77).

Phillip Kitcher in his book, *Vaulting Ambition: Sociobiology and the Quest for Human Nature,* has critiqued Wilson's analysis of the question of human freedom. He says that once all of the peripheral arguments, speculations, and elaborations are cleared away from Wilson's message that what we are left with is a rejection of human autonomy. He feels that this is a recapitulation of the traditional deterministic reactions to the question of free will. In that sense he thinks that Wilson has said nothing new. Kitcher reviews the fact that both genetic and cultural determinists have advanced the argument that all of our desires and intentions are imposed upon us and that, therefore, we are not free. According to cultural determinism, people are so molded by the effects of their environment that they are entirely the product of the influences to which they are exposed. Genetic determinists, on the other hand, emphasize the inherent rigidity of the organism. There is little that the environment can do, from this point of view, to modify the genetic character of the organism. From either perspective, Kitcher points out, the prospects of freedom based on choice and intention look very dim.

Kitcher says that if we can set aside the myths of both the blank mind and the iron hand of genetics the prospects of human freedom brighten. The image of both the formless creature, the blank slate, and the rival image of human beings as entirely reflexive organisms gives way to something quite different. Kitcher goes on to discuss the importance of the ways in which our dispositions to behavior vary with the environment. He says:

> If my choices are produced through my reflection on what would be best, if they are modifiable in light of new information about the consequences of my planned actions, then, although those choices are ultimately fixed by my genotype in the sequence of environments I encounter, they may nonetheless be free (Kitcher, 1985, p. 411).

As a part of a debate which followed the publication of Wilson's book, *Sociobiology,* Larry Miller wrote, "the dichotomy (genetics vs. environment) is a false one; both extremes present a passive view of humans as vehicles for either our genes or our environment. We view humans as active agents, striving to shape lives and destiny. Determinist theories, whether genetic or environmental serve to inculcate an ethos of passivity and thus render us susceptible to active manipulation by others" (Miller, 1976, p. 50).

One of the most important and compelling metaphors of human existence concerns our freedom. Freedom, after all, is basic to the manner in which we view ourselves. Freedom has been a goal throughout human history which has elicited great individual sacrifice, it is one that people have died for.

Grasping the concept of freedom means coming to understand the importance of the idea of free will or, the term I used earlier, intentionality. As René Dubos said of freedom in *Celebrations of Life:* "The greater the freedom of a particular organism to select where it goes, what it does and how it responds to stimuli, the more complex and more creative is the living experience" (1981, p. 38). Human beings have a great potential for freedom. We do, of course, change in response to the environment. That type of change is adaptive in character. We also change because of the unfolding of our genetic inheritance. That may be described as developmental change. These forms of change, of course, interact with one another. These factors, however, are given human character and definition by a third element or force. This is the potentiality which has been characterized through our examination of the lives of conjoined twins. Whether we call it free will, choice, self direction, or intentionality it is the creative element of human life which mediates between and within both heredity and environment. It is that capacity which makes human life more than the mere sum of deterministic thought and mechanistic action.

As Dubos further noted in his book, and as was cited in the early pages of this one, it is seemingly impossible to prove scientifically that human beings are innately free. People, however, are constantly acting as if freedom is an endowment in their lives, at least as a potential to be sought or fought for. To reject free will as an element of human life because it does not fit within the existing parameters of science is to dismiss its meaning also in political and social terms. To dismiss it in these terms is to reject our fundamental cultural and philosophical heritage.

The promotion of passivity in our thinking about ourselves and others is taken up by James Deese in his fascinating book entitled *American Freedom and the Social Sciences.* He argues that there are two influential and pervasive ideas which are competing to shape the future of our culture. One is the idea that all human actions are determined and controlled by the forces of heredity and environment. Deese believes that this is the assumption that is dominant in psychology, political science, economics, and other social sciences. The competing idea is the belief that human beings are capable of making free choices, undetermined by forces beyond their control. According to Deese, it is this idea that is the foundation of our form of government. He states that, "Without the notion of free choice, democracy is a black joke" (Deese, 1985, p. 3). He feels that these contradictory notions of human nature are on a "collision course" and that unless we become aware of the contradiction in the way we view ourselves and treat each other we will be discouraged and damaged by it.

Although we have seen that there are still "genetic radicals" and "blank slate extremists" who are plying their trades, most scientists have come to believe that heredity and environment cannot be separated. Thus the popularity of the interactionist point of view, the view that both factors interact to determine who we become. As most people involved with the issue have embraced the interactionist perspective, the idea that the nature/nurture controversy is waning has become quite popular. In fact, some feel that the debate is dead. However, as Richard Morris has stated, "If it is dead, it is a very lively corpse" (1983, p. 26). Even a cursory look at the literature reveals that strong genetic arguments are still being made. Equally true, is that environmental determinism is still quite pervasive both in the sciences and in social services. The nature/nurture controversy has not been resolved. The concepts of determinism and reductionism, of reducing human beings to simple organisms that are programmed in all of their actions, still reign in the arenas of *both* heredity and environment.

One of the few developmental theorists who has addressed the issue of self direction is Erik Erikson. Erikson, in discussing the psycho-analytic concept of ego, has pointed out that Freud did not invent the term. Rather the term was historically used to denote a unity of the body and soul. In philosophy it implied a degree of permanency and consistency in conscious experience. Erikson believes that an important function of the ego is to integrate experience in a way that lends centrality to being. It is through the concept of the ego that persons may be viewed as doers rather than "impotent sufferers." To quote Erikson, it is the vehicle of the ego which makes the person "Active and originating rather than inactivated . . . ; centered and inclusive rather than shunted to the periphery; selective rather than overwhelmed; aware rather than confounded; all of this amounts to a sense of being at home in one's time and place, and, somehow, of feeling chosen even as one chooses" (1982, p. 89). Erikson believes that it is through the individual "I" that we grow out of our earliest bodily experiences and out of our early instinctual development to the point where we can achieve a sense of orientation in the universe.

A major feature of Erikson's work, and one which has been largely overlooked, is his attempt to interrelate the different factors of the personality through the use of the term *ego*. Erikson transcends the usual dichotomy of heredity and environment. He argues that to truly understand an individual personality, we must use a system of "triple bookkeeping" (Erikson, 1963). His approach is essentially one of integration. He attempts to understand the complexity of heredity, environment, and self direction through this integrated viewpoint. He feels that we must understand these three factors *and* the intricate interaction that takes place among them in order to truly comprehend the human condition. A theme which is repeated throughout Erikson's book *Childhood and Society* is that to understand people we must look at all of the aspects that contribute to their construction as individuals. We must examine their biological realities, their social experience, but we must also attempt to understand the person's experience of self.

As I was exploring the challenging question that my study of conjoined twins had presented me, I found a book that I referred to in the previous chapter. In that book, *Not In Our Genes,* Richard Lewontin, Stephen Rose, and Leon Kamin make a powerful statement concerning the nature/nurture controversy. They explain that it is their view that the relationships between heredity and environment are complex in ways that have never been adequately encompassed by simple reductionist arguments. They believe that in the same way that hereditarian reductionism has misportrayed human beings as the mere products of genes, extreme cultural determinism has inaccurately portrayed people as simply the product of family circumstances, social class, and the random environmental events they have encountered. They feel that environmental determinism is just as wrong, indeed just as absurd, as biological determinism. Lewontin and his colleagues argue that both of these reductionistic approaches share an arithmetical fallacy: that the life of a human being can be partitioned neatly into a biological proportion and an environmental proportion, and that the sum of these proportions will equal 100 percent of what a life is about.

Lewontin, Rose, and Kamin observe that a move in the right direction was made by those who have advocated an interactionist model of human nature. They state, in fact, that "interactionism is the beginning of wisdom" (1984, p. 268). The interactionist model, as mentioned earlier, is based on the idea that what an organism is at any moment depends both upon the genes that it carries and on the environment in which the development of the organism is occurring. From this perspective organisms which are identical in genetic makeup but who develop in different environments may be just as different as two genetically discrete individuals. It is the unique interaction between heredity and environment in each individual case that determines the outcome, the product.

Although they see interactionism as a move in the correct direction they also consider it to be an insufficient model for understanding the human condition. A major flaw which they perceive in the interaction model is that it actually supposes an alienation between the organism and the environment. This alienation draws a clean line of demarcation between the organism and the environment and portrays the environment as acting upon the organism (and in this sense "interacting") while forgetting that the organism acts on the environment.

Lewontin, Rose, and Kamin feel that two powerful metaphors have characterized hereditarian and environmental theories. The first of these metaphors is that of development as a process of the "unfolding" of preexisting structures. This is the metaphor that underlies most stage theories of development and that sees human nature as the gradual emergence in a fixed sequence of that which is predetermined. Thus, this is the core of the biological determinism model. The second metaphor is one based on Darwinian theory; the metaphor of "trial and error." In this model organisms confront the environment and adapt to its realities, its demands. This metaphor lies at the core of the interaction model.

A feature that is common to both of these metaphors is that of the alienation between the organism and the environment. In the first case the organism, for the most part, develops oblivious to the conditions of the environment. In the second case it is only the organism that adapts and molds itself. The environment is static and makes demands. If the organism does not adapt it dies. Lewontin and his colleagues feel that this view of the alienation of the organism and the environment pervades psychology, biology, and philosophy. Yet, they state, it is simply wrong.

They offer a new model. They call this model "interpenetration."

From this perspective organisms themselves define their environment. Organisms do not simply adapt to previously existing conditions. Instead they are viewed as creating and transforming the world by their own actions. Lewontin and his colleagues believe that, "just as there is no organism without an environment, there is no environment without an organism" (1984, p. 273). From this perspective neither the organism nor the environment is a closed system. The organism is open to the environment and the environment is open to the organism.

The major theme of their discussion is that all organisms, but particularly human beings, are not simply the results of but are also the creators of their own environments to a significant degree. From this perspective, development is viewed as a process of codevelopment between the organism and its environment. This is particularly characteristic of human psychological development. At every juncture the developing mind, which is partially the consequence of past events and biological conditions, is also engaged in an active re-creation of the world in which it exists. Thus any serious account of psychological development must not only specify the influence of heredity and environment but how the individual penetrates these factors, how he or she creates environments. From this perspective we see the individual human being as actively interpreting the world, making choices, and, therefore, altering his or her own reality. Lewontin, Rose, and Kamin quote Marx, "The philosophers have only interpreted the world in various ways; the point, however, is to change it" (1984, p. 277).

In summarizing their conceptual position, Lewontin, Rose, and Kamin state that what is most characteristic of human development and of our behavior is that we are each the consequence of an immense array of interacting causes and factors. In speaking of freedom they stress that our actions are independent of any one of these factors. Thus, it is the intricate interplay of multiple factors and the interpretation we make of our experiences which in effect creates freedom. They argue that the essence of the difference between human biology and that of other organisms is the degree of this freedom. To quote them:

> Our brains, hands, and tongues have made us independent of many single major features of the external world. Our biology has made us into creatures who are constantly re-creating our own psychic and material environments, and whose individual lives are the outcomes of an extra-ordinary multiplicity of intersecting

causal pathways. Thus it is our biology that makes us free (ibid., p. 300).

What is the definition of being human? The rhetoric, if not always the reality, of our political and cultural tradition has made freedom a basic attribute and right of human life. It has been argued that it is freedom that makes us unique among other living organisms, and the protection of which should be the first cause of all government. Freedom. The right, the responsibility, the capacity to control one's own life. Freedom is such an integral part of our perception of what it means to be human that people who have difficulty demonstrating their freedom are often at risk for being devalued in our society. Poor people, old people, and handicapped people are often in danger of being considered less than human because of their diminished abilities to exercise personal freedom. It is a great irony that societal laws so often serve to protect those of us who need it least and deny equal protection to others exactly because their lessened capabilities for the exercise of free will cause them to need it the most. We often punish, in effect, what is considered inappropriate dependency. When people do not show that they are free, when they appear to be too dependent, their very right to live may be called into question.

A functional reality is that we expect human beings to be able to exercise free will. There is nothing more central to the question of human existence than being free—simply being free.

A sociological point of view that resonates well with this perspective is that of Dale Dannefer. Dannefer feels that there are three kinds of principles that are crucial to an adequate understanding of human development: the malleability of the human organism in relation to the environment; the structural complexity and diversity of the social environment; and the role of human intentionality as a mediating factor in development (1984, pp. 106-107). According to Dannefer nearly every major school of sociological thought has emphasized, in some way, the uniquely "open" or "unfinished" character of the human organism in relation to its environment. Although the organism may be most "open" in infancy and early childhood, there is growing evidence that it retains a remarkable plasticity throughout life. The organism is constituted as a human being in interaction with the environment, and is continually maintained and reordered in an ongoing way across the life course. Through this interaction characteristics, which may appear to passively emerge or "develop," are actively produced, sustained, or modified.

I have come to agree with Leon Eisenberg who said, "Man is his own chief product" (1978, p. 175). Eisenberg argues that the infant who becomes aware that he or she can control finger movements has already begun a process of self transformation from observer to actor. Adolescents who critically examine the conventional wisdom of their culture are "making" themselves into adults. Adults who expand their concerns beyond their families and beyond their own communities to humanity in general are constructing their own lives in more completeness.

Surely an individual's will may be overwhelmed by a harsh or threatening environment. Likewise a person handicapped by genetic misfortune may be unable to fully exercise self direction. Because of these realities it would be a mistake to view all individuals as completely responsible for their own lot in life. The results of this kind of blameful perspective could prove to be disastrous for individuals and for society. It is critical, however, that along with heredity and environment we recognize the *potential* for intention and purposefulness in each human life.

Some would argue vigorously that freedom is not a suitable topic for examination in the light of science. Even those who might agree that freedom is one of the quintessential philosophical questions of human life could oppose the discussion of freedom in scientific terms and they would be well within the boundaries of orthodox thought on the suitable applications of science. It is curious that a concept for which people have been willing to die, the idea of freedom, would not be seen as a substantial enough matter for the tradition and methodology of science. Increasingly, however, there are voices being raised that question the usually accepted parameters of science and the confidence placed in its orthodox methodology. Lewis Thomas, for example, has expressed misgivings about the certainty invested in "scientific" findings. In his book *The Medusa and the Snail* he explains, "The only solid piece of scientific truth about which I feel totally confident is that we are profoundly ignorant about nature" (1979, p. 73). Also addressing the limits of science as it has traditionally been defined, Merleau-Ponty commented on the importance of an expanded scientific vision:

I cannot shut myself up within the realm of science. All my knowledge of the world, even my scientific knowledge, is gained from my own particular point of view, or from some experience of the world without which the symbols of science would be meaningless. The whole universe of science is built upon the world as directly experienced, and if we want to subject science itself to rigorous scrutiny and arrive at a precise assessment of its meaning and scope, we must begin by reawakening the basic experience of the world of which science is the second order of expression (1962, p. viii).

In her article entitled "Constructing Psychology: Making Facts and Fables for Our Times," Sandra Scarr discusses the idea that facts always exist within a theoretical and social context. The human mind also, according to Scarr, must be viewed within a social context. Its understandings are in part created by the social and cultural universe in which it exists. Knowledge of the world, a world view if you will, is always constructed by the mind according to working models of reality. In this sense, argues Scarr, we do not discover facts or scientific data; we invent them. The facts and data that we invent depend upon our perceptions, the perceptions of others who influence us, and what these perceptions lead us to search for.

One view of science is that it is a distribution of ideas that has continued to evolve through competition (Toulmin, 1973). The evolution of ideas does not, however, imply that one single view will always dominate. On the contrary, evolution implies change. Scarr posits that because many ideas are available to us and do in fact compete, we need not choose a single lens through which to view the world. Rather, she says, we can "enjoy a kaleidoscope of perspectives" (Scarr, 1985, p. 511). Quoting from her article:

In our own intellectual population we should construct the richest account we can of human behavior, which will include variables from several levels of analysis and alternative theoretical accounts. Because we do construct science and reality, we might as well give it breadth, depth, and some excitement (ibid.).

Scarr closes her article by saying that this approach to science frees us to think what has not been thought before, even the unthinkable by traditional standards. It seems to be her belief that our scientific point of view and where we look for facts should be constrained only by imagination and what she calls "a few precious rules of the scientific game" (ibid., p. 512).

In this book I have attempted to adhere to "a few precious rules" while approaching a difficult question in an unorthodox way. The lives of conjoined twins provided me with a different lens through which to view the idea of human freedom. I believe that the perspective I found through that lens is rich and intriguing. Learning of the realities in the lives of the twins has reinforced for me the belief that the premise that human development and behavior is determined only by the chemistry of nature and nurture is fallacious. It has strengthened my conviction that each of us has the potential to live a life of purpose and choice. It has confirmed my faith in freedom.

REFERENCES

Dannefer, D. (1984). Adult development and social theory: A paradigmatic reappraisal. *American Sociological Review, 49* (1), 100-116.

Deese, J. (1985). *American freedom and the social sciences.* New York: Columbia University Press.

Dubos, R. (1981). *Celebrations of life.* New York: McGraw-Hill.

Eisenberg, L. (1978). The "human" nature of human nature. In *The sociobiology debate.* New York: Harper and Row.

Erikson, E. (1963). *Childhood and society.* New York: W. W. Norton.

_____. (1982). *The life cycle completed.* New York: W. W. Norton.

Howard, G. (1985). The role of values in the science of psychology. *American Psychologist, 40* (3), 255-65.

Kitcher, P. (1985). *Vaulting ambition: Sociobiology and the quest for human nature.* Cambridge, MA: The MIT Press.

Lewontin, R., Rose, S., & Kamin, C. (1984). *Not in our genes.* New York: Pantheon Books.

Merleau-Ponty, M. (1962). *Phenomenology of perception.* London: Routledge and Kegan Paul.

Miller, L. (1976). Sociobiology: The debate continues. *The Hastings Center report* (vol. 6, pp. 48-50).

Morris, R. (1983). *Evolution and human nature.* New York: Seaview/Putnam.

Scarr, S. (1985). Constructing psychology: Making facts and fables for our times. *American Psychologist, 40* (5), 499-512.

Thomas, L. (1979). *The Medusa and the snail.* New York: Viking Press. Press.

Toulmin, S. (1973). *Human understanding*. Chicago: University of Chicago Press.

Wilson, E. O. (1978). *On human nature*. Cambridge, MA: Harvard University Press.

Index

About the Author

J. DAVID SMITH is a professor of education and human development at Lynchburg College in Virginia. He received undergraduate and graduate degrees from Virginia Commonwealth University. He earned his doctorate at Columbia University. A former Peace Corps volunteer, Dr. Smith has also been a special education teacher and a counselor. He is the author of *Minds Made Feeble* (1985) and *The Other Voices: Profiles of Women in the History of Special Education* (1987), as well as numerous articles that have appeared in professional and academic journals. Dr. Smith and his wife, Joyce, are the parents of three children.

ATE DUE